The Weekend Cook

Angela Hartnett

with lots of help from Neil Borthwick,
friends and neighbours

First and foremost I would like to dedicate this book to Pat, a very dear, much missed, kind, generous and funny friend – times together were always great fun.

To my husband Neil, without whom this book could not have been written, and finally to friends and family because quite frankly there is nothing more important in life than those two groups of people.

The Weekend Cook

Good food for real life

Angela Hartnett

with lots of help from Neil Borthwick,
friends and neighbours

with photography by
Jonathan Lovekin

BLOOMSBURY ABSOLUTE
LONDON · OXFORD · NEW YORK · NEW DELHI · SYDNEY

Contents

Introduction

I have been living in East London for over 20 years. It's a top community with wonderful neighbours who are also friends, one of whom was the late legendary television producer, Pat Llewellyn, who was not only a great friend and close neighbour, but also a keen cook and wonderful host. Pat famously produced *Two Fat Ladies*, Gordon Ramsay's *Kitchen Nightmares* and discovered a baby-faced Jamie Oliver – need I say more!

Pat used to say that I made entertaining at home look easy, and it was she who first suggested I should write a book about the joy of quality time spent with friends and neighbours. And if Pat said something, you listened.

I've been cooking professionally for over 30 years and it's a job that I love. The hours are long, though, and the sight of the weekend ahead is something I look forward to with relish.

The weekend is a time to put your working life into perspective and to reconnect with friends and family. And what better way to rebalance your work/life priorities than around the kitchen table, sharing good food and delicious wine with people who bring smiles and fun into your home. It may sound like a busman's holiday but I genuinely enjoy having people over. It also means that at the end of the evening I just need to travel upstairs to my welcoming bed, rather than find a cab to take me back home across London.

My husband Neil and I love entertaining. Over the years we have hosted family birthday parties, street parties – including cooking for 600 friends and neighbours at the Queen's Golden Jubilee street party – five-course truffle lunches, lunches for two Michelin-starred chefs that featured the world's largest turbot – well, it seemed like it – Burns Night bashes, simple lunches, hangover breakfasts,

come-back-to-our-house-after-a-night-at-the-pub suppers and all types of celebrations in between.

Of course, cooking at home is entirely different to the experience of working in busy restaurant kitchens. When I'm at the restaurants, I'm cooking for other people, so every plate has to be perfect. But when I'm at home, I'm cooking for myself, and with the radio on and a glass of wine on the go, I find it relaxing, a world away from work. I want to cook meals at home where I don't have to worry about fancy presentation. I want great flavours and simple recipes, satisfying one-pot dishes that give me time to talk to my friends, rather than complicated recipes that mean I have to keep clattering down the stairs to our basement kitchen to stir something.

In this book you will find all my go-to recipes that have served me well over the years when cooking for fun at home. Some of the recipes in the book come from our friends and neighbours, with whom we've shared many evenings and many bottles of wine. Many are inspired by other chefs and wonderful food writers.

I think my love for entertaining must come from my Italian background, where any excuse to get around a table as a family to eat and have fun was joyfully taken. Nonna set the standard, and anyone who came over to our house was always offered something delicious to eat. It's the standard that I have kept to – no matter how many come to our house in East London, expected or out of the blue, we will feed them and fun will be had.

I'm an informal host and I will often text people on the day to see if they want to come round for something to eat. Over the course of the photoshoot for this book, I'd often text neighbours to find out who was free and then invite them over to eat all the food we'd just cooked. I've done the same when clearing out the freezer!

Keeping it simple is the key to enjoyable entertaining. A cold starter, bowls of pasta, roast chicken, plates of charcuterie, a good cheeseboard – these are the sorts of dishes that keep things fun and remove the stress of having people over.

Our basement kitchen at home is pretty basic, and nothing remotely like the high-end kitchens that Neil and I work in during the week. It's quite a small kitchen with few work surfaces and hardly any kit. But if you have a set of decent knives and just one good work surface then all will be fine.

Many of the recipes in the book can be prepared in advance, and some will even taste better the next day. I hate waste, so a lot of the recipes in this book use classic store cupboard ingredients – see the cupboard spaghetti on page 124 or the griddled monkfish tails with harissa marinade on page 102 as perfect examples of this.

Some things, of course, take time to get right, but once perfected you'll never look back.

An example that I always quote is soup. Soup, much like a quiche, is actually quite hard to make, something many chefs don't realise. A good soup is all about the base. Take the time to make the best stock. A good soup shouldn't have all the ingredients just shoved together in a pan, boiled up, liquidised and then plonked on the table. A good soup builds layers of complexity – roasting your veg or bones, making your own stock and then finishing it with the

final layers of flavour. There is more to a good soup than many think and the extra effort is well worth it.

There are always tricks and cheats with smart hosting to save time. And sometimes there are potential disasters to be averted! I love a great gazpacho and I was planning to make a batch when family and friends were coming over one Sunday lunch. I had left things to the last minute, as I normally do, and had simply run out of time. I had to run to a local supermarket and buy up all their cartons of gazpacho. I marinated a bunch of tomatoes to accompany the gazpacho and served the soup up with style and shameless pride. But pride comes before a fall and unfortunately in our house the kitchen is downstairs and we eat upstairs so people always end up helping me clear the plates. My friend Liz, on opening the dishwasher to load the soup bowls, discovered all the plastic supermarket gazpacho containers and asked mischievously whether it was sadder that I'd lied to my mother, my brother and my sister about making the soup, or that I had kept all the containers.

In many ways this book is about the importance of community. The East End, where I live, is constantly changing. It's quite different today than when I moved in 21 years ago. But what hasn't changed, and what makes the area so special for me, is the people.

People think of London as huge and anonymous, unfriendly and frantically busy. But that is not the case where I live in Spitalfields. We've all known each other for a long time, and people look after one another, something which became increasingly evident over the course of the recent pandemic. During that period we would swap things over doorsteps and fences, and we all came outside on Christmas Day to raise a glass to toast the season. Early in the first lockdown, Neil and I drove around delivering baskets of loaves from St. John Bread and Wine – a great local restaurant – to make sure it didn't go to waste.

But it didn't just take a pandemic to receive the support of our loving community. When Neil had a bad accident a few years ago, we were cared for by our neighbours, who regularly popped round to help out or bring us food. Sandra, our local pub landlady, was round every single day just to see if she could do anything to help with food packages in order to feed all the visitors, as she said that I didn't have time to cook. Sometimes where we live feels more like a small Italian village in the heart of London, or a small Welsh village as Pat used to say. I couldn't and wouldn't want to live anywhere else in this city.

Our street has seen a number of increasingly festival-like street parties over the years, organised by the Spitalfields Society and Spitalfields Community. We've had three so far, and we keep talking about having another one for the Queen's Platinum Jubilee. They're lots of fun and bring everyone together. Because of the position of our house, everything sort of centres around us. The bar is always outside our front door and we do most of the food – thanks to my sister Anne who was on the committee and keeps volunteering us!

Beyond that, we have our community traditions. Ben always hosts a Christmas Eve party, John and Kate have a party on the Sunday before Christmas, and we host a Burns Night supper. So some of the dishes in the book come from my neighbours as well as from me or Neil. See the chapter from pages 170 to 199 for these lovely recipes.

Sandra, the landlady of our local, The Golden Heart, is the linchpin of the community; she knows everyone and everyone knows her. We're very fortunate to have such a great local on our doorstep, and it is very much the heart of the community. If I lose my keys, the pub is where I go to wait until Neil gets home. I'm fortunate in that every time I pop in, I know someone to talk to. But it's not easy to get out once you're inside, so sometimes you just have to be tough with yourself and resist popping in for a drink as it will never be quick!

Close to The Golden Heart is the wonderful St. John Bread and Wine, another of our go-to places. Often during a quiet supper at Bread and Wine, we'll bump into some neighbours, and then the night takes a turn and we'll end up at the pub until the small hours, with more friends joining.

The history of Spitalfields is remarkable. Immigrant communities have come in and been welcomed, enriched the area and moved on – Huguenots, Jews and Bangladeshis in particular. This remarkable history still remains visible in the area, with many of the buildings inspired by the Huguenots who built so much. One of our neighbours even has a small Jewish place of worship in his back garden. Sadly, some of the physical history is being removed with the drive towards gentrification, and, writing as a chef, some of the best old curry houses along Brick Lane are being out-priced and are having to move on. Which is, I suppose, one of the prices we pay for living in London.

I believe that any recipe is just a guide. If you want to change or tweak them, that's fine. If you want more spice or you don't like lemon, then add or take out as you want. Some of my recipe introductions offer ideas for ways you could take a recipe and add other flavourings or ingredients, but you may well have your own ideas too. Taste as you go and cook for your preferences and palate.

A lot of the recipes in the book can be mixed and matched as you want. So, you could serve some of the vegetable dishes alongside the meat or fish dishes, or perhaps use the vegetable recipes as an array of small plates for a delicious vegetarian tapas selection.

Most importantly, all the recipes in this book are easy and delicious. And though they are usually served in our house on weekends, they will work just as well for midweek lunches and suppers. The only essential ingredients are friends and family and lots of them.

Happy cooking, and happy eating!

Starters

Confit Garlic and Goat's Curd Toast

This is an original 'Hoppy' (Simon Hopkinson) recipe that I used to serve as canapés on little toasts when I was cooking at the Whitechapel Gallery. Neil adapted the recipe for The French House in Soho, where he serves it on slabs of toast.

The secret to a great confit garlic is to use the best olive oil and the freshest garlic. You could add thyme or rosemary and any left over will keep in the fridge. It's also great slathered on rib-eye steak or squeezed over grilled fish.

Serves 4

4 new-season garlic bulbs
olive oil
sea-salt flakes

To serve
4 slices of white sourdough
    bread
150g goat's curd
a small handful of chopped
    flat-leaf parsley (leaves
    and stems)

Slice the tops (just over halfway up) from the 4 bulbs of garlic. Reserve the tops for sauces or vinaigrette at a later date.

In a pan large enough to hold the garlic tightly together, add 1 tablespoon of olive oil. Place the pan over a low heat, season the heads of garlic with sea salt, and place them cut-side downwards in the pan, moving them around the pan gently so that they colour evenly, for about 4–5 minutes, until golden brown.

When the garlic bulbs are ready, turn them over and cover them with oil. Turn down the heat to very low and gently confit the garlic for about 45 minutes, until it is completely soft when you squeeze it. Leave it to cool in the oil.

To serve, toast the sourdough slices on both sides. Spread the toast with goat's curd and sprinkle it with a touch of sea salt. Sit a confit garlic bulb at one end of each slice of toast and sprinkle everything with the parsley. Suggest to your guests that they squeeze the garlic over the bread before eating.

Beetroot and Lentils

I always set out to the local greengrocer with the best of intentions, aiming to buy some veg thinking I'll be really healthy that week. So, I buy loads of wonderful vegetables that just sit in the fridge. And Neil will despair and end up turning these forgotten vegetables into gorgeous salads. He is quite brilliant at taking whatever we have to hand and making something great. I'm always inspired by the way Neil cooks.

For this recipe we like to use puy lentils, but any lentils would work. Roasting the beetroot in the oven along with the herbs, sugar, salt and a generous amount of vinegar almost pickles the beetroot as it cooks.

Serves 4

500g beetroot
2 garlic cloves, crushed
2 thyme sprigs
1 teaspoon light brown
    soft sugar
½ teaspoon sea salt
115ml red wine vinegar
100ml extra-virgin olive oil
½ teaspoon Dijon mustard
200g puy lentils
a handful of flat-leaf
    parsley, leaves and stems
    finely chopped
freshly ground black
    pepper

Preheat the oven to 180°C/160°C fan/Gas 4. Line a large oven tray with foil, leaving enough overhang that you will be able to wrap the foil over the top and the edges will meet in the middle to seal.

Place the beetroot, half the garlic and half the thyme, along with all the sugar and salt, in the foil-lined tray, and add 100ml of the red wine vinegar. Close the foil to form a pillow and then pour 500ml of water into the tray around the outside of the foil.

Bake the beetroot for 40 minutes, until a knife goes easily through the largest beetroot.

While the beetroot are cooking, make the vinaigrette. Mix the oil, remaining vinegar and mustard together, then season well with pepper and leave to one side.

When the beetroot are ready, allow them to cool slightly, then remove them from the tray while still warm. Using a small knife, peel away the outer skins and cut each beetroot into quarters. Add the beetroot pieces to the vinaigrette and leave them to marinate for 2 minutes.

Cook the lentils for about 30 minutes, until al dente, or according to the packet instructions, adding the remaining garlic and thyme to the cooking water. Allow the lentils to cool a little in the cooking water, then drain them, discarding the thyme and garlic.

Toss the lentils into the beetroot, then add the flat-leaf parsley and toss again. Serve warm.

Baked Leeks with Egg and Mustard Vinaigrette

We made this most recently for our friend and neighbour Basil on his birthday, when we had about 14 people over to celebrate the great day. It's full of my favourite things – capers, Dijon mustard, anchovies, vinegar and herbs – and is served with perfectly blanched leeks and soft-boiled eggs. It's wonderful!

Serves 4

2 bunches of baby leeks, or 2 large leeks
3 eggs
2 teaspoons Dijon mustard
20ml white wine vinegar
60ml extra-virgin olive oil
a handful of lovage, leaves picked and chopped (use tarragon if you can't find lovage)
a handful of chives, chopped
2 anchovies, drained and chopped
1 teaspoon capers, drained and chopped
salt and freshly ground black pepper

Top and tail the baby leeks and soak them in water to remove any grit. If you're using large leeks, trim off the dark green tops and slice them into 2cm rounds.

Bring a pan of salted water to the boil over a high heat. Add the leeks and boil for 5 minutes, until just tender. Remove using a slotted spoon and set aside. Leave the pan on the heat.

Add the eggs and cook on a low boil for 6 minutes, until soft boiled. Drain the eggs and transfer them to a bowl of iced or very cold water to stop the cooking process. Set them aside until cooled.

Meanwhile, combine the mustard, vinegar and olive oil in a large bowl.

Peel the cooled eggs and roughly chop them. Add the chopped eggs to the dressing in the bowl and season well, especially with black pepper. Add the chopped herbs, anchovies and capers, and mix well.

To serve, place the leeks on a serving plate and pour over the egg and mustard vinaigrette.

Fried Ceps and Eggs

This for me is the perfect wild mushroom recipe. When we're cooking at our restaurant at Lime Wood we go out and forage for the ceps with the dogs. We can get trumpette, but I prefer ceps and girolles, and in the height of wild mushroom season they're the absolute best. If unavailable you could use dried and rehydrate them. If you're using dried mushrooms, the water used for soaking them can then be used to flavour other dishes. Serve with lots of buttered toast.

Serves 2

50g unsalted butter, plus
    a little extra for frying
    the eggs
3 tablespoons olive oil
6 large, firm ceps, wiped
    clean, stalks trimmed,
    then thickly sliced
a handful (about 200g) of
    chestnut mushrooms,
    wiped clean and stalks
    trimmed
a handful of wild garlic
    or spinach
2 eggs
warm buttered toast,
    to serve
sea salt and freshly ground
    black pepper

Place a large frying pan over a medium heat. When hot, add the butter and olive oil and when the butter starts to bubble up, add the ceps. Fry the ceps, turning, so that they colour on both sides (about 3 minutes on each side), then add the chestnut mushrooms and continue to cook for another 2 minutes.

Add the wild garlic and a touch more butter. Gently move the mushrooms in the pan to create two gaps and when the butter starts to bubble, crack the eggs into the gaps. Turn off the heat and leave the eggs to cook in the heat of the pan until the whites are set and the yolks are still runny (about 3 minutes). Season and serve on the buttered toast.

Fried Artichokes and Sage

I really came to love artichokes when I was first working in Italy as an au pair. The *nonna* would get some beautiful, spindly artichokes and fry them quickly in the pan so that they kept their natural colour, and they were so, so delicious. When I worked with Gordon, he'd make a delicious artichoke soup, which I loved. But my preference is to simply soak and then fry the artichokes, as in this recipe, and serve with some sage leaves on the side.

Serves 2

4 violet artichokes
juice of 1 lemon
4 tablespoons plain flour, seasoned with salt and pepper
750ml groundnut oil
10 sage leaves
lemon wedges, to serve
sea salt and freshly ground black pepper

Clean the artichokes by cutting away the tough outer leaves. With a curved paring knife, carefully cut off the purple part of each leaf. Peel off the outer skin of the artichoke stems and carefully tidy up the base by peeling it neatly with a vegetable peeler.

Pour enough water into a bowl to enable you to immerse the artichokes. Stir through the lemon juice. Add the artichokes and leave them submerged for at least 10 minutes, then remove them from the water and drain them thoroughly. Toss them in the seasoned flour.

Pour the oil into a deep saucepan so that it comes no more than two thirds of the way up the sides. Place the pan over a medium heat and heat the oil to 140–150°C on a cooking thermometer, or until a cube of bread browns in 30 seconds.

Using a slotted spoon, immerse the artichokes in the hot oil and allow them to fry for 10 minutes, until golden and tender. To check if the artichokes are cooked, pierce the base of one of them with a knife – if it goes through easily, they are ready.

Carefully remove the artichokes from the oil and transfer them to a plate lined with kitchen paper to drain off the excess oil. Season well while still warm.

Allow the oil to come back up to temperature, then add the sage leaves and fry them for 30 seconds–1 minute, until crisp. Remove them from the oil and set aside to drain on kitchen paper.

Serve the artichokes and sage leaves with lemon wedges for squeezing over.

Pumpkin, Pear and Walnut Salad

This is my Italian version of a classic Waldorf salad. The trick is to buy a good pumpkin in season. I like to use an Ironbark or a good Delica pumpkin, both of which are nice and dense and not as watery as many of the ones you might find in the local supermarket.

You could substitute hazelnuts or almonds for the walnuts, or whatever you have in the cupboard.

Serves 2 as a main
or 4 as a starter

1 x 400g pumpkin, deseeded
75ml extra-virgin olive oil, plus extra for sprinkling
½ teaspoon Dijon mustard
½ teaspoon runny honey
2 tablespoons red wine vinegar
50g walnuts, toasted and roughly chopped
2 ripe pears, thinly sliced
½ small radicchio or red gem lettuce, leaves separated
sea salt

Heat the oven to 200°C/180°C fan/Gas 6.

Cut the pumpkin into 2.5cm chunks – the skin should be tender enough that you can leave it on and eat it, but if it seems tough and inedible, peel the pumpkin, then cut the flesh into chunks.

Place the pumpkin on an ovenproof tray, sprinkle with a little olive oil and season with salt, then bake it for 35–40 minutes, until tender.

Make a vinaigrette. Combine the 75ml of olive oil with the mustard, honey and vinegar in a small bowl and then stir through the walnuts and set aside.

Allow the cooked pumpkin to cool slightly and transfer it to a plate. Pour half the walnut dressing over while the pumpkin is still warm.

Mix the rest of the vinaigrette with the pears and radicchio and toss them together to make the salad. Arrange the pear and radicchio salad on a serving dish with the pumpkin, and serve.

Mozzarella and Pickled Radicchio

I have adapted this recipe from my mate James Ferguson. He used to cook it at the Towpath Cafe on London's Regent's Canal, where he served the mozzarella with some lovely pickled radicchio and pangrattato breadcrumbs, and it was delicious. You had the gentle softness of the cheese and the silkiness of the radicchio with a lovely toasty crunch on top.

  We buy all of our cheese from The Ham & Cheese Co. in Bermondsey. For this recipe I would always pick a buffalo mozzarella over a burrata.

Serves 4–6

200ml white wine vinegar
200g caster sugar
a pinch of white
    peppercorns, crushed
a pinch of coriander seeds,
    crushed
1 whole radicchio, cut into
    8 slices
about 25g salted butter
100g panko breadcrumbs
a pinch of thyme leaves
a pinch of chilli flakes
4 x 125g buffalo mozzarella
    balls
extra-virgin olive oil,
    for drizzling
sea salt and freshly ground
    black pepper

Put the vinegar, sugar, peppercorns and coriander seeds in a pan with 200ml of water. Place the pan over a high heat and bring the liquid to the boil to dissolve the sugar. Remove from the heat.

Lay the slices of radicchio on a tray and drain the hot pickling liquid through a sieve over the top. (Discard the contents of the sieve.) Allow to cool, turning the leaves from time to time as they do so.

Add the butter to a frying pan and place over a medium heat. As the butter starts to melt, add the breadcrumbs, thyme and chilli flakes. Season and toast until golden brown, stirring all the time as the breadcrumbs cook quite quickly. Remove the pan from the heat.

To serve, scatter the radicchio over a serving plate. Tear the mozzarella over the top and season with salt and pepper. Drizzle with olive oil, then scatter over the toasted breadcrumbs. Serve immediately.

Radishes and Anchovy Mayonnaise

This is really a nibble rather than a starter. As part of a well-intentioned health kick I'll often buy a load of radishes to serve with a classic anchoïade – a kind of anchovy mayonnaise.

We tend to always have tinned anchovies, eggs and garlic in the house, making this a really quick recipe to throw together. Sometimes, when we're hosting friends, I just do a main and serve the radishes as an easy dip before we sit down to eat, perhaps with some olives or a plate of really good charcuterie.

Any veg would be great to dip here, celery, carrots or fennel perhaps – whatever you have to hand.

Makes 400g

2 egg yolks
½ teaspoon Dijon mustard
a squeeze of lemon juice,
    plus extra if needed
10 anchovies in olive oil,
    finely chopped, oil
    reserved
up to 250ml sunflower oil
a small handful of flat-leaf
    parsley leaves, finely
    chopped
2 bunches of radishes
    with leaves, thoroughly
    washed and drained
salt and freshly ground
    black pepper

In a large bowl (ideally one with a rounded base), add the egg yolks, mustard and lemon juice and whisk together.

Measure the olive oil from the anchovies in a jug and top it up with the sunflower oil to make 250ml altogether.

Then, drop by drop, start pouring the oil into the bowl with the egg mixture, whisking all the time. Gradually increase the amount of oil you're adding, building up to a slow trickle and whisking continuously as you do so, until you have a lovely, thick mayonnaise. Check the seasoning and add a touch more lemon juice, or a little salt or pepper, if needed.

Stir in the chopped parsley and the anchovies and mix well. Serve the radishes with the mayonnaise on the side.

Puntarella with Anchovy Mayonnaise

Puntarella is a very seasonal type of Italian chicory. It has tough leaves and a tough stalk and can take a punchy anchovy dressing. It's quite hard to find so you might need to hunt it out at your local greengrocers. If you can't find any puntarella then the recipe would work with common chicory – just don't over-dress it as it's more tender than the puntarella.

This is the same anchovy mayonnaise as for the globe artichokes and radishes (see pages 158 and 46) – it's one of my favourites and very versatile.

Serves 6

1 puntarella
4 tablespoons anchovy
    mayonnaise (see page 46)

Prepare the puntarella by removing the green leaves and cutting the stalks at an angle. Wash lightly and dry in a salad spinner.

Slice the roots and wash and dry them in a salad spinner.

Place the leaves and roots in a bowl and add 4 tablespoons of the anchovy dressing. Mix well. Owing to the saltiness of the dressing, there's no need to season. Serve immediately – this is perfect with roast chicken.

Crab Salad

I know I'm very fortunate to have great suppliers and great chef friends. Seafood guru Mitch Tonks often sends us crabs up from Devon and sometimes we get them sent to our door from Portland Shellfish. We have so much crab here in the UK yet so often our catches are sent abroad. We should be eating more crab – it is just so delicious and a wonderful thing to enjoy with friends.

This salad could be either a great starter or a fantastic main event with bowls of fries. This is not the classic crab salad with egg and parsley but a sea-fresh crab salad with a lovely hit of lime. You could replace the baby gem with chicory or kohlrabi, or a mix of the three would be great. And homemade mayonnaise of course!

Serves 4

400g white crab meat
a large bowl of ice
juice of 1$\frac{1}{2}$ limes
2 baby gem lettuce, leaves
    separated
3 tablespoons extra-virgin
    olive oil
a handful each of basil,
    mint and coriander,
    leaves and tender stems
    picked and chopped
salt and freshly ground
    black pepper

For the mayonnaise
1 egg yolk
1 tablespoon white wine
    vinegar
$\frac{1}{2}$ teaspoon Dijon mustard
300ml vegetable oil
150g brown crab meat
$\frac{1}{2}$ lime

First, make the mayonnaise. Put the egg yolk, vinegar and mustard in a food processor and blitz lightly to combine. Little by little, add the oil through the feed tube, mixing continuously as you do so, until the mixture emulsifies to form a loose mayonnaise. Add the brown crab meat and blitz the mixture together. Season with salt and pepper to taste, and add a good squeeze of lime juice. Transfer the mixture to a bowl and set aside.

Sit the white crab meat on a plate set into the bowl of ice and gradually pick through it to make sure there are no pieces of shell. Season with salt and pepper and a touch of lime juice.

Mix the salad leaves with the olive oil and remaining lime juice, then spread them across a large serving dish. Add the crab meat, dotting it all over the salad leaves. Sprinkle over the herbs and serve with the mayonnaise on the side.

Mackerel Tartar

If there's an occasion where you want to impress, then this is a lovely restaurant-style dish that can be done at home. It's easy to prepare ahead of time because the fish is cured by the other ingredients. The freshest of fish is essential and if you can't get mackerel almost off the boat then use very fresh sea bream or seabass, both of which work really well.

You could also experiment with different vinegars for curing the fish in place of the citrus.

Serves 2 as a
generous starter

½ cucumber, peeled, halved lengthways and deseeded
1 small red onion, finely chopped
juice and finely grated zest of 1 unwaxed lime
1 teaspoon baby capers
1 tablespoon chopped dill
2 tablespoons crème fraîche
2 super-fresh mackerel fillets, skins removed
a large bowl of ice
4 thin slices of rye bread, to serve
sea salt and freshly ground black pepper

Slice the peeled, deseeded cucumber halves very thinly into half-moons. Place the slices in a colander set over a bowl and season with salt. Leave the cucumber like this for about 30 minutes to draw out the moisture.

Using your hands, wring out as much of the remaining water from the salted cucumber as you can.

Place the red onion in a large bowl. Add the lime juice and zest, along with the capers, cucumber slices, dill and crème fraîche. Season with black pepper and set aside.

Dice the mackerel fillets into small cubes and transfer them to a clean bowl set inside the large bowl of ice. Stir in the onion and cucumber mixture to mix lightly, then leave the tartar in the fridge to chill for a good 15 minutes before serving.

To serve, toast the slices of rye bread under a hot grill until crisp. Divide the slices between two plates and serve the tartar alongside.

Soups

Potato and Wild Garlic Soup

The potatoes in this recipe give the soup the volume you need, whilst the wild garlic, watercress and chives provide the hit of flavour. This is a bit of a cheffy soup as wild garlic can be quite hard to find, but it's a great pairing with potatoes and well worth trying to hunt down. Wild garlic is actually quite easy to find for free in springtime when walking in the countryside. You could use celery leaves or lovage when it's in season in place of the chives; it's perfect for this soup.

Serves 4

15g unsalted butter
1 small onion, finely sliced
3 potatoes, peeled and cut
    into 2cm cubes
1 litre vegetable stock
about 75g watercress,
    finely chopped
about 150g wild garlic,
    roughly chopped
100ml double cream
½ bunch chives, roughly
    chopped
extra-virgin olive oil,
    to serve
sea salt and freshly ground
    black pepper

Melt the butter gently in a large pan over a low heat. Add the onion, season and allow the onion to sweat for about 5 minutes, until it begins to soften. Add the potatoes and cover with the stock. Cook for 15 minutes, until the potatoes are tender, then add the watercress and wild garlic, cooking for about 3 minutes, until wilted.

While the soup is cooking, gently whip the cream, season with salt and pepper and stir in the chives. Leave the flavoured cream in the fridge until you're ready to serve.

Remove the soup from the heat and, using a hand-held stick blender, blitz until smooth. Serve immediately in bowls, drizzled with olive oil and with a spoonful or two of whipped chive cream on top.

Summer Vegetable Soup

Here I've used courgettes, peas, broad beans and asparagus – all beautiful veggies, but use whatever veg you have to hand. The trick is to lightly sauté the vegetables so that they retain their greenness. Don't overcook them.

Use a good vegetable broth or a chicken stock. Some shop-bought stocks are pretty good – just be sure to buy the best you can and be aware that they're often a bit saltier than a homemade stock.

Serves 6

1 tablespoon olive oil, plus extra to serve
½ small onion, finely chopped
1 garlic clove, finely chopped
1 celery stick, diced
100g fresh peas, podded
100g fresh broad beans, podded
1 courgette, diced
4 asparagus, woody ends discarded, and cut into 2cm slices
1.2 litres vegetable stock
a handful of mixed herbs, such as basil, mint and flat-leaf parsley, leaves and tender stems lightly chopped
sea salt and freshly ground black pepper

Heat the oil in a large pan over a medium heat. When hot, add the onion, garlic and celery, season and lightly sauté for about 10 minutes, until the onion is soft but not coloured.

Add the peas, broad beans, courgette and asparagus and sauté for 3 minutes, then season with salt and pepper. Add the stock to cover the vegetables and bring the liquid to the boil. Cook for about 4 minutes, until the vegetables are just tender. Stir in the herbs and a good glug of olive oil, then serve immediately.

Cock-a-leekie Soup

I've never known why prunes are traditionally included in this soup. I imagine it's to add a certain sweetness, and they're absolutely delicious. If you didn't have any prunes, you could use sultanas or medjool dates to add the sweetness.

This is my go-to soup when I'm feeling ill, as I think chicken-based soups all feel so restorative.

After roasting a chicken I never throw away the bones but freeze them, and then when I have enough I make a good broth.

Serves 6

1 medium chicken (about 1.4kg), cut into 8 pieces
1 large carrot, peeled and cut into large dice
1 celery stick, cut into large dice
1 onion, quartered
1 bay leaf
150g pearl barley, rinsed
1 leek, finely sliced
50g soft, dried prunes, chopped, to serve
sea salt and freshly ground black pepper

Put the chicken in a large pan with 2 litres of cold water. Place over a high heat, bring the water to the boil, then reduce the heat to a simmer. Skim away any residue that has risen to the surface of the liquid.

Add the diced vegetables, the onion quarters and the bay leaf, season with salt and pepper, and cook at a low simmer for $1^{1}/_{2}$–2 hours, until you have a lovely, tasty stock.

Strain the stock into a separate pan. Reserve the chicken and set aside, but discard the vegetables. Place the stock on a medium heat, add the pearl barley and sliced leek, and allow to simmer for 25–30 minutes, until the barley and leeks are tender.

While the barley is cooking, shred the chicken meat, discarding the bones and skin, and add the meat back into the soup base once the barley and leeks are cooked.

To serve, divide the chopped prunes equally between your serving bowls. Ladle over the soup, making sure the chicken and leeks are equally divided between each bowl, and serve immediately.

Artichoke Soup

My neighbours John and Sandy, who have an amazing allotment and bring us artichokes every year, are the inspiration for this recipe. I regularly come home to find a box of just-harvested artichokes plonked outside the front door. Scrub them clean keeping the skin on, then slice them and pair with loads of onions. Again, as always, it's all about the base layer. The soup is rich and delicious and perfect to enjoy on its own.

Serves 4

50g unsalted butter
a splash of olive oil
1 small onion, sliced
2 garlic cloves, chopped
500g Jerusalem artichokes, unpeeled, scrubbed until clean, then chopped into rough chunks
600ml chicken or vegetable stock
a splash of single cream (optional)
roasted chestnuts, chopped, to serve (optional)
soft-poached egg, to serve (optional)
sea salt and freshly ground black pepper

Heat the butter and oil together in a large pan over a low heat. When hot, add the onion and garlic, season with salt and pepper, and cook for 5 minutes, until the onion is soft but not coloured.

Add the artichoke chunks and cook for 5 minutes, turning occasionally, then pour in the stock. Bring the liquid to the boil, then reduce the heat to a simmer. Season again and cook on a low simmer for 30 minutes, until the artichokes are soft.

Remove the soup from the heat and blitz it using a hand-held stick blender, or in batches in a food processor, until smooth. Pour the soup back into the pan and check the seasoning. If your soup is too thick, add the splash of cream – you're looking for the consistency of pouring double cream.

Return the soup to a low heat and warm it through until piping hot. Serve sprinkled with some roasted chestnuts or, for real luxury, serve topped with a soft-poached egg, if you wish.

Cullen Skink

Both this and the cock-a-leekie soup (see page 60) are a result of us hosting Burns Night suppers at home. And what can beat a classic Scottish soup. The traditional base is smoked haddock, but another smoked fish would work just as well. I love making this soup – it's so delicious and easy to make, and so hard to get wrong. Just be sure that you use good smoked haddock.

Serves 4–6

500g undyed smoked haddock, skin on
1 bay leaf
15g unsalted butter
1 onion, peeled and finely chopped
1 leek, sliced lengthways, then sliced thinly into half-moons
2 potatoes, peeled and cut into 1cm dice
400ml whole milk
1 tablespoon chopped chives
a small handful of flat-leaf parsley, leaves and stems, chopped
sea salt and white pepper

Put the haddock and bay leaf in a pan and cover with 300ml of cold water. Season with white pepper and bring the liquid to the boil over a high heat. Reduce the heat to a simmer and poach the haddock for 5 minutes, until just cooked through, then remove the pan from the heat.

Remove the haddock from the poaching liquid and transfer it to a plate. You should be able to easily remove the haddock flesh from the skin. Flake the flesh into pieces and then leave it to cool (discard the skin).

Pour the poaching liquid into a measuring jug and set aside.

Melt the butter in another pan over a medium heat. Add the onion and sweat for 3 minutes, then add the leek and season. Sweat for a further 2–3 minutes to soften the leek, then add the diced potato and a touch more salt. Add the reserved poaching liquid. Lower the heat, cover the pan with a lid and cook the vegetables for 10 minutes, until the potatoes are soft but not mushy.

Remove a quarter of the potato and leek mixture from the pan and leave it to one side. Add half the flaked haddock and the milk to the pan and heat through. Remove the pan from the heat and, using a hand-held stick blender or by pouring the soup into a food processor or blender, blitz until smooth.

To serve, return the soup to a gentle heat until hot. Divide the reserved potato and leek mixture and the remaining flaked haddock between the bowls and pour over equal amounts of the soup. Finish with the chopped chives and parsley and serve immediately.

Lamb Broth

We used to serve this at the Merchants Tavern in Shoreditch and it was very popular. If you've cooked a leg or shoulder of lamb for lunch or supper then just use the bones and trimmings to make a great base broth for the soup. Deglaze the cooking pan, keeping all the juices for the stock and you will have yourself the best base for the best soup. You can use lamb, hogget or mutton for this but hogget is perfect.

Serves 6

1kg lamb bones
2 litres chicken stock
1 garlic bulb, plus 2 finely sliced garlic cloves
1 onion, plus 1 small, finely diced onion
2 tablespoons olive oil
2 carrots, peeled and diced
1 celery stick, diced
1 small turnip, diced
sea salt and freshly ground black pepper

Preheat the oven to 200°C/180°C fan/Gas 6.

Tip the lamb bones into a large roasting tin and roast for 20 minutes, turning them occasionally so they colour evenly, until golden brown and the fat has rendered. Drain off the fat (you can reserve it for cooking roast potatoes another time, if you wish).

Place the bones in a large pan and cover them with the chicken stock. Add the garlic bulb and whole onion and season with salt and pepper. Place the pan over a medium heat and cook the bones for 2 hours, skimming off any scum that rises to the surface and topping up with water if the stock reduces too much (you don't want the liquid to reduce by more than one third).

Remove the pan from the heat and leave the broth to sit for 30 minutes before you pass it through a colander into a bowl or jug. Then, pour it through a fine sieve into a clean jug. Pick any meat from the bones left in the colander and sieve and set aside. Discard the bones.

Heat the olive oil in a large pan over a medium heat. When hot, add the diced onion, carrot, celery and turnip. Sauté for 5 minutes, adding the sliced garlic for the last 2 minutes of the cooking time, until the vegetables start to soften.

Pour in the strained broth and cook over a medium heat for 10–15 minutes, to allow the flavours to develop, then add the picked meat, stir through, season with black pepper and serve in bowls.

Meat

Neil's Sunday Chicken

For a while at home, we found ourselves having roast chicken at lunch every Sunday. It got to the stage when even my sister, who comes over a lot, said that it was becoming ridiculous and 'can we have something else for a change'. But our roast chicken is delicious and this is a wonderfully simple way to cook it. Once cooked you just put the whole roasting dish on the table for everyone to dig in and help themselves. It's also a great way to use up any vegetables in the fridge – just make the time to sweat them off gently.

For something a bit different and Moroccan in feel you could add some preserved lemon and coat the chicken in harissa, and use more onion and garlic and fewer carrots.

Serves 4

1 whole chicken, skin-on, cut into 8 pieces
olive oil
25g salted butter
3 carrots, peeled and cut into large chunks
2 onions, peeled and quartered
3 celery sticks, cut into large chunks
1 bulb of garlic, smashed
a few rosemary sprigs
1 lemon, quartered
a handful of flat-leaf parsley, leaves and stems chopped
sea salt and freshly ground black pepper

Preheat the oven to 200°C/180°C fan/Gas 6.

Season the chicken pieces all over with salt and pepper and set aside.

Heat a touch of oil and the butter in a large pan over a medium heat. When the butter starts to bubble, add the chicken skin-side downwards and sear for 10 minutes, until golden brown and crispy. Remove the chicken from the pan and set aside.

Pour a good dash of olive oil into a large roasting dish. Add all the vegetables, including the smashed garlic bulb, season with salt and pepper, and add the rosemary sprigs and lemon quarters. Place the chicken on top.

Roast for 50 minutes, until the chicken and vegetables are cooked through, then allow to rest for 10 minutes and finish with the chopped parsley. To serve, take the roasting dish to the table and allow everyone to help themselves.

Poached Chicken with Summer Vegetables

When entertaining you often just want brilliant flavours from a simple recipe and this poached chicken fits the bill perfectly. Buy the best chicken you can and poach it in water, no other liquid, along with fresh vegetables, allowing the wonderful fat of the chicken to flavour the finished dish. Simple. Don't mess with this recipe.

Serves 6

1 whole chicken (about 1.5–2kg)
2 carrots, peeled and cut into large chunks
2 celery sticks, cut into large chunks
1 white onion, quartered
1 small garlic bulb, halved horizontally
2 thyme sprigs
15g salted butter
a handful of flat-leaf parsley, chopped

For the summer vegetables

1 bunch (about 400g) of asparagus
200g peas in their pods
200g broad beans in their pods
extra-virgin olive oil
a few mint leaves
sea salt

Place the chicken in a large pan and cover it with cold water. Place the pan over a medium heat and bring the liquid to a slow boil, then immediately reduce the liquid to a simmer. Skim any residue from the top. Add the vegetables and thyme and cook for 50–60 minutes at a low simmer, until the chicken is cooked through.

Shortly before the chicken is ready, prepare the summer vegetables. Snap the wooden stalks from the asparagus stems and pod the peas and broad beans.

In a pan of boiling salted water, add the asparagus and cook for 1 minute, then add the broad beans and peas and cook for a further 3 minutes, until everything is tender. Remove the vegetables from the pan using a slotted spoon and set them aside in a bowl. Add a drizzle of olive oil, some picked mint leaves and a touch of sea salt.

When the chicken is ready, using a slotted spoon, drain the chicken and vegetables, transferring them to a serving dish.

Take a few ladlefuls of the stock and pour them into a small pan (you can keep any leftover stock in the freezer to use in soups and risottos). Place the pan over a medium heat and leave the stock to reduce for 3 minutes, until slightly thickened. Add the butter and the flat-leaf parsley, stir to combine to a sauce, then pour the sauce over the poached chicken and vegetables.

Chicken Pie

I came up with this recipe for a friend's birthday and I have to say it's pretty good. Why? Because you use the juiciest part of the chicken – the thighs – along with English mustard. The mustard gives it a kick but you could use Worcestershire sauce or Tabasco, or even sriracha if you wanted to mix your cuisines. Another good alternative would be a spoon of horseradish cream. As ever, it's about a confident cook experimenting and riffing on a tried and tested theme. Leeks, carrots and mushrooms work really nicely in a chicken pie and if you have some good bacon or pancetta then throw it in. A pie is a great way to use things up!

Good puff pastry is vital here and I have no problem with shop-bought – just use a good brand. I really think that everyone should stop being so snobbish about shop-bought pastry.

I once made a chicken pie for friends and rolled out the pastry far too thick. When I took it out of the oven the pastry underneath was still raw so we quickly sliced the crispy bit off the top, removed the raw bit underneath, popped the crispy bit back on the pie and no one was any the wiser.

And you can't beat some boiled frozen peas on the side!

Serves 6

8 skinless bone-in chicken thighs
200g chestnut mushrooms
2 bay leaves
750ml hot chicken stock, plus extra (or a little white wine) if needed
2 celery sticks, chopped into 2cm pieces
2 carrots, peeled and chopped into 2cm rounds
2 leeks, sliced into 1cm rounds
1 tablespoon olive oil
1 small onion, finely chopped
50g salted butter
50g plain flour
150ml crème fraîche
½ teaspoon mustard powder
½ a bunch of tarragon leaves, chopped (about 2 tablespoons)

Put the chicken thighs, mushrooms and bay leaves into a large saucepan. Pour over the stock and season well. Place the pan over a medium–high heat and bring the liquid to the boil. Cover with a lid, reduce the heat and simmer for 25 minutes, until the chicken thighs are cooked and tender. Set aside to cool.

While the chicken is cooking, in a separate saucepan of boiling salted water, boil the celery and carrots for about 5 minutes, until they are tender. Use a slotted spoon to remove the celery and carrots and transfer them to a bowl. Add the leeks to the same cooking water and boil for about 5 minutes, until tender. Drain and set aside to cool.

Once the chicken has cooled, remove the thighs from the stock and tear the meat from the bones, pulling it off in bite-sized pieces and transferring it to a bowl as you go.

Pour the chicken stock through a sieve, reserving it in a large jug. You should have about 500ml. If you don't have enough, make up the volume with a little extra chicken stock from a stock cube, or with white wine.

Heat the oil in a large saucepan over a low heat. When hot, add the onion, season with salt and pepper and fry

320g sheet of ready-rolled
    puff pastry
1 egg, beaten
sea salt and freshly ground
    black pepper

for 10 minutes, until the onion is softened but has not taken on any colour.

Add the butter and stir until melted, then add the flour and stir to form a smooth paste. A little at a time, pour the reserved stock into the paste, whisking as you go. Keep whisking over a medium heat, until the mixture has thickened to a smooth sauce consistency.

Stir in the crème fraîche and mustard powder, then add the chicken, celery, carrots, leeks and finally the tarragon, stirring everything through to evenly combine. Season to taste.

Spoon the filling into a 2-litre ovenproof pie dish and level the top. Leave until cool, then cover and refrigerate for 30 minutes.

Preheat the oven to 200°C/180°C fan/Gas 6.

While the filling is in the fridge, prepare the pastry. On a lightly floured work surface, unfurl the pastry sheet, and roll it if necessary to about 3mm thick, making sure it will fit over the pie dish with about a 2cm overhang.

Remove the chilled filling from the fridge. Brush the edge of the pie dish with the beaten egg and gently transfer the pastry lid over the top, pressing around the edges to seal. Trim to neaten and use the trimmings to add a 1cm border around the edge of the pie, which will help prevent shrinkage.

Brush the pastry with the remaining beaten egg and make an incision in the middle of the pie with a sharp knife to let out the steam. Bake for 30 minutes, until the pastry is golden and the filling is bubbling hot.

Roasted Lamb Shoulder with Tomatoes

Though I'm not the greatest fan of lamb, sometimes you just can't beat a roast shoulder served family-style. I like to serve this with a big green salad on the side too, but you could beef the vegetables up a bit and make a classic ratatouille to serve alongside which would give a nice Provençal feel.

A lovely extra to this recipe is to add some diced potatoes to the roasting tin 40 minutes before the end of the cooking time, allowing them to roast in the lamb fat and juices.

Serves 6

2.25kg whole lamb shoulder, skin on
olive oil
8 garlic cloves, sliced
2 rosemary sprigs, torn into small pieces
2 onions, quartered
4 plum tomatoes, halved
a glass of white wine (about 175ml)
sea salt and freshly ground black pepper

Heat the oven to 220°C/200°C fan/Gas 7.

Place the lamb, skin-side up, on a board. Using a sharp knife, make some small slits through the skin, rub the lamb with some olive oil, then insert the garlic and rosemary into the slits. Season with salt and pepper.

Place the lamb in a roasting tin and roast for about 20 minutes, until browned. Reduce the oven temperature to 160°C/140°C fan/Gas 2–3.

Transfer the lamb to a plate, place the onions and tomatoes into the roasting tin and place the lamb back on top. Add the wine to the tin.

Cover the lamb with foil, place the roasting tin back in the oven and roast the lamb for $3\frac{1}{2}$–4 hours, or until the meat is completely tender and coming away from the bone.

Leave to rest (still covered) for 20 minutes before carving and serving.

Remove the vegetables from the roasting tin and leave them to one side. Remove any excess fat from the roasting juices, then pour the juices into a pan and place the pan over a medium heat. Bring to the boil and reduce for about 20 minutes to thicken to a gravy consistency or until it coats the back of a spoon.

Serve the lamb with spoonfuls of the onions and tomatoes and the gravy for pouring over. And with a fresh, green salad or cauliflower cheese on the side, depending on the season and your mood.

Lamb Stew

This is basically a French-Italian lamb stew. It's great to make in volume to feed a hungry crowd. Lamb neck has become quite fashionable and is really delicious when cooked with a tomato base. I really like that all the veg you cook with you then eat – carrots, celery, onion, garlic – the whole shebang.

If you don't want to use lamb neck you could substitute shoulder or any cut that has fat in it; in fact, any cut that is a hard-working bit of the animal. Hogget or mutton would be good too. You could add tinned chickpeas halfway through cooking for extra bulk and texture.

Serves 8

2 tablespoons olive oil
4 lamb neck fillets, halved, fat on
2 carrots, peeled and cut into 2cm chunks
2 celery sticks, each cut into 6 pieces
1 garlic bulb, halved horizontally
2 heaped teaspoons tomato purée
1 bottle of dry white wine
1 litre hot chicken stock
cooked polenta, to serve
sea salt and freshly ground black pepper

Preheat the oven to 160°C/140°C fan/Gas 2–3.

Pour the oil into a large flame- and ovenproof dish (one big enough to hold all the ingredients). Place this over a medium heat. Season the neck fillets and add them to the dish, turning them frequently for about 5–7 minutes, until they are a nice, even colour all over.

Remove the meat from the pan and set aside. Add the vegetables and sauté them for 5 minutes, stirring frequently, until evenly coloured. Add the tomato purée and cook for 3 minutes. Return the lamb to the pan and pour over the wine. Leave the liquid to bubble away for 5 minutes, or until the volume has reduced by half.

Pour over the stock and cut a piece of baking paper to the size of the pan, run it under cold water, then place it over the top of the stew. Put the lid on the pan. Cook the stew in the oven for 90 minutes, until the meat is cooked through and tender enough to pierce easily with the handle of a spoon.

If the sauce feels too loose when you remove the meat from the oven, drain it into another pan, leaving the meat and vegetables in the casserole pan covered with the baking paper. Place the sauce over a low heat and leave it to reduce until it has thickened to your liking. Serve the stew with polenta.

Roasted Pork Belly

This is a recipe inspired by Valentine Warner, a very good chef and food writer, and a friend who I adore. I was due to be cooking at a dinner at a festival a few years ago where all the recipes were pork and I was flicking through recipe books for inspiration. I loved the sound of Valentine's recipe – he basically smashed lemon into pork belly with rosemary and then roasted it. Now it's my go-to way of making pork belly. I probably add a bit more garlic to mine, along with thyme sometimes. It's just such a good and simple way to add great flavour.

Pork belly is a pleasingly cheap cut of meat and wonderfully easy to cook; you just need to get your oven temperatures right.

Serves 4

3 rosemary sprigs, leaves picked and finely chopped
finely grated zest of 2 unwaxed lemons
1 tablespoon fennel seeds
4 garlic cloves, peeled and crushed
2 tablespoons groundnut oil
1.5kg pork belly, skin on
sea salt and freshly ground black pepper

Heat the oven to 220°C/200°C fan/Gas 7.

Put the rosemary, lemon zest, fennel seeds and garlic in a mortar and grind them with a pestle to a good paste. Stir in the oil and season with salt and pepper, then set aside.

Pat the pork belly dry with kitchen paper, then using a sharp knife, score across the narrow width of the belly at 2cm intervals, taking care to score through the skin and fat, but not into the meat. Rub the rosemary and lemon marinade all over the scored skin.

Pour 1cm depth of water into a roasting tray, place a rack in the tray and the pork belly on top. Roast in the oven until the skin starts to bubble and crackle; this should take about 30 minutes. Then, reduce the heat to 160°C/140°C fan/Gas 2–3 and cook for a further 1 hour, until the meat is tender to the point of a knife. If the pork needs crisping up, increase the oven heat to 240°C/220°C fan/Gas 9 and roast for a final 15 minutes, until it's good and crispy.

Remove the pork from the oven, leave it to rest for 10–15 minutes, then slice and serve. I like to serve it on a bed of leaves for some freshness.

Braised Pork Cheeks with Mustard

I used not to cook pork cheeks, but Luke Holder, who is the executive chef at Lime Wood, cooks with them a lot. I really like what he does with them so I have become a convert and have taken inspiration from Luke. This is my celebration of pork cheeks. I just sauté the veg and then braise the meat slowly with good stock and wine.

Serves 6

12 pig cheeks
2 tablespoons plain flour, seasoned with salt and black pepper
4 tablespoons olive oil
15g unsalted butter
1 onion, finely chopped
2 leeks, finely chopped
1 bay leaf
5 thyme sprigs, leaves stripped
200ml dry white wine
200ml chicken stock
1 tablespoon wholegrain mustard
100ml double cream
a bunch of crime di rapa or tenderstem broccoli, steamed, to serve
sea salt and freshly ground black pepper

Dust the pig cheeks in the seasoned flour. Heat half the oil in a large, heavy-based casserole with a tight-fitting lid. Add the cheeks and cook them over a medium heat for 2–3 minutes each side, until browned (you'll need to do this in batches). Remove with a slotted spoon and set aside.

Melt the butter in the pan with the remaining oil. Add the onion, leeks, bay leaf and thyme and fry over a low heat for 20 minutes, until the vegetables are soft. Return the meat to the pan and pour in the wine and stock. Season with salt and pepper, increase the heat and bring the liquid to the boil. Reduce the heat to low again, cover the casserole with the lid and simmer for $2^{1}/_{2}$ hours, until the cheeks are tender.

Remove the meat from the casserole, set it aside and keep it warm. Increase the heat, bring the sauce to the boil, add the mustard and cream and bubble for 5–10 minutes, until you have a rich, golden sauce. Return the pig cheeks to the casserole to warm through, then serve immediately with the crime di rapa or tenderstem broccoli.

Osso Bucco with Risotto Milanese

This is a favourite classic dish from the Lombardy region of Italy, and one that features on the Café Murano menus in winter. It's packed full of flavour and guaranteed to impress. If you have time, you can make the osso bucco a day ahead and gently reheat it when you want to serve. I always find that this allows the flavours to develop and intensify, making it even more delicious. Finish with gremolata to cut through the richness of the dish.

Serves 4

For the osso bucco
a little vegetable oil,
    for frying
4 veal shanks
2 carrots, diced
1 onion, quartered
1 celery stick, sliced
1 thyme sprig
1 rosemary sprig
1 garlic bulb, halved
    horizontally
1 tablespoon tomato purée
250ml white wine
1 litre chicken stock and
    500ml veal stock (or use
    1.5 litres chicken stock)

For the risotto
3 tablespoons vegetable oil
2 shallots, finely chopped
2 garlic cloves, finely
    chopped
400g carnaroli risotto rice
100g salted butter, cubed
300ml white wine
1.5 litres hot vegetable
    stock
good pinch of saffron
50g Parmesan, grated
salt and freshly ground
    black pepper

First, prepare the osso bucco. Heat a little vegetable oil in a saucepan over a medium heat. Place the veal shanks in the pan and brown them all over, then remove them and set them aside on a plate.

Add your carrots, onions and celery to the pan, and sauté for 5 minutes, then add the thyme and rosemary and the garlic halves and continue to sauté for another 3 minutes. Add the tomato purée, and allow it to cook for 3 minutes, stirring as you do. Deglaze the pan with the white wine, scraping up the goodness from the bottom and allowing the liquid to reduce by about half.

Return the veal to the pan, and cover it with both of the stocks. Bring the liquid to a simmer, cover the surface with baking paper and leave everything to simmer over a low–medium heat for about 1 hour, until the meat falls off the bone.

To prepare the risotto, heat the vegetable oil in a large heavy-bottomed saucepan over a medium heat. When hot, add the shallots and garlic and sauté for about 5 minutes, until softened but not coloured. Add the rice, then add a couple of cubes of butter. Toast the rice for 2 minutes, stirring all the time. Add the white wine and allow it to evaporate.

Lightly season the rice with salt and pepper and then start to add the hot vegetable stock, ladleful by ladleful, allowing the rice to absorb each addition before pouring in the next. After about 7–8 minutes, add the saffron, then keep adding the stock. Stir continuously throughout. When you're coming up to about 17 minutes, and your rice is cooked, pull the pan off the heat, and stir through the remaining cubed butter and the Parmesan. Serve immediately with your osso bucco and a generous helping of the sauce on top.

Braised Oxtail

This is a beautiful winter dish. Don't mess around with it or try to be clever, however if you want a little extra edge then Ed Schneider, a great food and travel writer and friend, once brought me some dried smoked peppers as a gift when he came to stay – adding one of these gives a great kick to the dish. Finish with parsley or mint, and if the dish feels too rich, add a dash of sherry vinegar to cut through the richness and round this dish off.

Serves 4–6

olive oil
15g salted butter
2kg oxtail, cut into chunks
    by your butcher
3 carrots, cut into 4cm
    chunks
2 celery sticks, cut into
    4cm chunks
2 onions, quartered
1 garlic bulb, quartered
    and unpeeled
1 thyme sprig
1 bay leaf
1 tablespoon tomato purée
1 bottle (750ml) of good-
    quality red wine
300ml chicken stock
a handful of flat-leaf
    parsley (about 15g),
    leaves and stalks
    chopped, to serve
cooked polenta or boiled
    potatoes, to serve
    (optional)
sea salt and freshly ground
    black pepper

Heat the oven to 150°C/130°C fan/Gas 2.

Add a good glug of olive oil and the butter to a large, ovenproof casserole or saucepan (it needs to be big enough to hold the oxtail) and place it over a medium heat until the butter has melted and starts to bubble.

Season the oxtail with a good twist of black pepper and salt, and add the meat to the pan. Allow it to brown for 8–10 minutes, turning occasionally until evenly coloured all over. Do this in batches so the oxtail colours nicely.

Remove the meat from the pan using a slotted spoon and set it aside on a plate. Add the vegetables, including the garlic, and the herbs to the pan and allow the vegetables to colour for about 10 minutes. Add the tomato purée and cook for 3 minutes, stirring continuously.

Add the oxtail back into the pan, then add the wine. Allow the liquid to reduce for about 10 minutes over a medium heat, until the meat is glazed, then pour in the chicken stock.

Cover the casserole with a lid and transfer it to the oven. Cook the oxtail for 3 hours, until the meat comes away from the bone. As braised oxtail is even better the next day, set the cooked stew aside and allow it to cool, overnight if possible.

To serve, gently reheat the stew over a low heat for 20–30 minutes, until it starts to bubble and is piping hot. Stir in the parsley. Serve with cooked polenta or boiled potatoes on the side.

Faggots

Faggots are basically an English meatball and they're so good. My faggot recipe is inspired by Neil, Nigel and Val, three top chefs, and I've adapted their recipes and here is mine.

The caul can be a faff but if you're going to do this dish properly then you need to do the caul too – sorry! It will be worth it though. I remember Nigel Slater eating Neil's at his restaurant – he could not get enough of them.

Serves 6

200g beef caul (from your butcher)
50g unsalted butter, plus extra for frying
1 onion, finely chopped
1 tablespoon chopped thyme leaves
10 sage leaves, finely chopped
1 teaspoon ground mace
400g pork belly mince (from your butcher)
100g bacon mince (from your butcher)
6 lambs' kidneys, rinsed, deskinned, cored and chopped
100g lamb's liver, chopped
100g stale white bread, blitzed to coarse breadcrumbs
75ml whole milk
mashed swede, to serve
sea salt and freshly ground black pepper

Place the caul in a bowl of cold water, cover and refrigerate. Leave it to soak overnight.

When you're ready, make the faggot mixture. Melt the butter in a frying pan over a low heat. Add the onion, thyme, sage and mace and cook over a medium–low heat for a good 10 minutes, until the onion is very soft but not coloured.

Place the pork, bacon, kidneys and liver in a bowl and add the onion mixture. Mix together well, then add the breadcrumbs and milk and mix again to combine.

Heat a dry frying pan over a medium heat and fry a little of the mixture until cooked. Taste for seasoning and adjust the mixture as necessary.

Divide the mixture into 12 equal pieces, rolling each piece into a ball. Place the balls on a baking tray and refrigerate them for about 15 minutes to firm up.

Remove the caul from the water and gently open it up where there are any holes and spread it out on your work surface. Take one faggot and fold the caul over the top of the faggot so it's tightly and completely covered, with the ends of the caul overlapping to seal. Cut away and trim off any excess caul. Place the faggot back on the tray, seal downwards. Repeat for all the faggots.

Heat some more butter in a frying pan over a low–medium heat. In batches, fry the faggots, seal downwards, for about 4 minutes, until they are browned, but taking care not to let them burn. Turn them over and gently fry on the other side so they are sealed (they shouldn't open, but if they do,

For the onion gravy

2 large onions, finely sliced
1 tablespoon dark brown
   soft sugar
2 tablespoons red wine
   vinegar
1½ tablespoons plain flour
dash of soy sauce
½ teaspoon Bovril
500ml beef stock

turning them will help to seal them). Transfer each batch to a baking tray while you repeat until all the faggots are good and brown.

In the same frying pan, make the gravy. Fry the onions in the leftover faggot fat over a low–medium heat for 30 minutes or so, until richly coloured. Add the sugar and vinegar and cook until the vinegar has evaporated completely. Then, sprinkle in the flour and cook gently, stirring, for a further minute or so, taking care not to burn the flour. Add the soy sauce and Bovril, then start adding the beef stock, bit by bit, stirring continuously, until you have added it all. Check for seasoning.

Add the faggots back into the pan, cover with a lid and cook over a low heat for 40 minutes, until the faggots are cooked through and you have a lovely, thick gravy. Turn the faggots gently during the cooking time. Serve with mashed swede.

Fish

Seabass, Orange and Fennel Crudo

This is a beautifully clean recipe – the freshest of fish, a bit of spicing and the acidic fruit to cure. If you don't have orange to hand, lime or lemon will do – you just need the acidity of the citrus to work its magic. If you cannot get hold of bass use seabream or monkfish. The key to this dish is to slice the fish nice and thin.

Serves 6 as a starter

500g skinless seabass fillet
½ teaspoon pink
    peppercorns, lightly
    crushed
2 tablespoons extra-virgin
    olive oil
2 blood oranges, segmented
    with any juice reserved
100g fennel, thinly sliced
    using a mandolin
a handful of your choice
    of herbs, leaves picked
    (I like to use dill or basil)
sea salt

Using a sharp knife, slice the seabass down the centre, then across at an angle so that it looks like sashimi.

Place the seabass pieces on a serving dish, season with the pink peppercorns and some sea salt and cover with the olive oil and orange juice. Top with the orange segments, sliced fennel and the dill and serve immediately.

Griddled Monkfish Tails with Harissa Marinade

This is dish that came about through clearing the fridge and using up the last of the jar of harissa. Mix the harissa with olive oil and some lime juice and spread it all over the fish, keeping some aside as a vinaigrette dressing to serve at the table. Perfect to cook on a smoking hot griddle pan or barbecue.

Serves 4

4 tablespoons harissa paste
2 tablespoons olive oil, plus extra for griddling the fish
juice and finely grated zest of 2 limes
4 filleted monkfish tails (about 200g each, prepared weight)
a handful of coriander, chopped

Mix together the harissa paste, olive oil, lime zest and three-quarters of the lime juice in a bowl to create a marinade. Using a pastry brush, brush the fish tails all over with the marinade and leave to marinate for 30 minutes.

When you're ready to cook, heat a griddle pan until hot. Add a touch of oil, then immediately add the monkfish tails and griddle for 3 minutes on either side.

Remove the monkfish tails from the pan, then sprinkle over the remaining lime juice and the coriander. Serve immediately with any extra marinade to drizzle over.

Red Mullet and Tomato

Red mullet is my favourite fish. I use the whole fish for this recipe. The garlic, chilli and tomatoes cook away gently to form the bed of the dish, then just pop the mullet on top of the vegetables to cook. When it's ready place the cooking pan onto the table and let everyone get on with it. This is a great recipe for sharing.

Serves 2

olive oil
1 garlic clove, finely chopped
1 dried peperoncino, crushed, or a pinch of chilli flakes
200g cherry tomatoes, halved
2 whole red mullet (about 200g each)
125ml dry white wine
a handful of basil leaves
a handful of flat-leaf parsley, leaves picked and chopped
2 slices of focaccia or white sourdough, toasted, to serve
sea salt and freshly ground black pepper

Heat a good glug of olive oil in a large, deep-frying pan over a low heat. Add the garlic and chilli and lightly sauté for about 1 minute, until the garlic is soft but not coloured. Add the tomatoes and cook for 15 minutes, until softened.

Season the red mullet and place them on top of the tomatoes. Add the white wine, cover with baking paper or a lid and cook for 3 minutes, then turn the fish over and cook for a further 3 minutes, until a skewer can go easily through the thickest part.

To serve, transfer the fish on to your serving plates, spoon the tomatoes over the fish, add the herbs and serve with the toasted bread on the side, drizzled with the juices.

Grilled John Dory

John Dory is a wonderful fish and one of the easiest to work with. It's also a great barbecue fish as it can take the heat from the coals – just add salt and pepper and slash the skin a bit. It can also take the flavours from both summer veg and winter veg, so it's a great all-year-round fish. And as it's so meaty it can welcome flavours like anchovy, capers and harissa.

This recipe uses piles of courgettes and tomatoes drizzled in oil and loads of herbs, roasted until soft with the John Dory popped on top.

Serves 4

1 tablespoon olive oil
1 garlic clove, sliced
4 plum tomatoes, halved
  and seasoned
1 small onion, peeled and
  quartered
2 courgettes, sliced into
  1cm pieces at an angle
a pinch of dried chilli
a pinch of chopped
  rosemary
a handful of basil, leaves
  picked
2 whole John Dory
  (800g–1kg each)
sea salt and freshly ground
  black pepper

Heat the oven to 180°C/160°C fan/Gas mark 4.

Place a large, ovenproof pan over a low heat. Add the olive oil and garlic and sauté for a few minutes, until the garlic is softened but not coloured. Add the tomatoes, onion, courgettes, chilli and rosemary.

Place the pan in the oven for 25 minutes, stirring occasionally, until the courgettes are cooked and the tomatoes have started to shrivel. Remove from the oven, stir through the basil leaves and keep warm.

Heat the grill to a very high heat.

Place the whole John Dory on a large chopping board and remove the eyes (or ask your fishmonger to do this). With a sharp knife, score the flesh at 2.5cm intervals across each fish. Season well, then place the two fish on a grill pan and grill for about 5 minutes on each side, turning once during cooking, until the flesh is opaque and cooked through. Serve the fish whole with the roasted vegetables on the side.

Mackerel with Red Cabbage

This dish was inspired by Fergus Henderson. We live just around the corner from St. John Bread and Wine – my most frequented restaurant in London. I'm always bumping into neighbours there; it has a wonderful community feel. What might start as a quiet evening at Bread and Wine usually ends up as a raucous night at The Golden Heart! St. John's do a smoked mackerel with horseradish, and an amazing red cabbage salad with beetroot and crème fraîche. I've sort of adapted both and brought them together.

The lovely vinaigrette cuts through the fattiness of the mackerel and will cure the cabbage and really enhance the flavours when left in the fridge for a few hours or overnight, so I suggest you begin this recipe the day before you intend to serve it.

Mackerel is always best at its freshest, so if you can't get the freshest of mackerel then smoked or pickled mackerel will work here too.

Serves 2 with leftovers

2 raw whole beetroot, peeled
½ red cabbage, finely sliced
75ml extra-virgin olive oil, plus extra for brushing
20ml red wine vinegar
1 teaspoon Dijon mustard
2 whole mackerel (about 300g each), gutted, but left whole and scored lightly
1 Granny Smith apple
a handful of flat-leaf parsley, leaves and stems chopped
sea salt and freshly ground black pepper

Using a mandoline, finely slice the beetroot into discs – take care with your fingers. Make small piles of the beetroot slices and, with a sharp knife, cut the beetroot into thin strips.

Add the beetroot strips to a bowl with the cabbage, then add the oil, vinegar and mustard and season well. Mix to combine, then cover, place in the fridge and leave the salad for at least 2 hours, but ideally overnight, for the flavours to combine.

To cook the mackerel, heat a grill pan over a high heat (or even on a barbecue) until roasting hot. Season the mackerel and lightly brush them with olive oil.

Add the fish to the hot pan, and leave them to cook for about 3 minutes – do not try to move them. Once the skins gets crispy and start to colour, turn the mackerel over (they should move easily) and cook them on the other side for about another 3 minutes, until cooked through. You can test when the fish is cooked by sliding a skewer through the thicker part, close to the head – if it goes in easily, the fish is ready. (There's nothing wrong with the mackerel being slightly undercooked at this point – the residual heat will carry on cooking them.)

While the mackerel is cooking, core the apple and slice it finely. Add the apple slices and the parsley to the beetroot and cabbage mixture and stir to combine. Serve the mackerel with the beetroot, cabbage and apple salad alongside.

Whole Trout with Almond and Herb Stuffing

We cooked this dish after Neil had been out fishing and had caught a fresh-water trout. It's the stuffing that makes this such a delicious dish; just soften onions and garlic in butter and mix it with the breadcrumbs, fresh herbs, almonds and slices of lemon. Trout is quite forgiving so you can use any mix of herbs you fancy.

The stuffing would work just as well with a whole salmon or with small sea breams or seabass.

I really like cooking fish *en papillote*, and you could certainly use the sealed paper technique here – just cut a big sheet of baking paper to line the oven tray. Once the fish is in and drizzled with the oil, gently bring the sides together, being careful not to wrap the fish too tightly, then crimp to seal and cook as per the instructions below.

Serves 2

25g salted butter
1 small onion, finely
  chopped
1 garlic clove, finely
  chopped
200g fresh breadcrumbs
1 tablespoon chopped sage
  leaves
a small handful of flat-leaf
  parsley, leaves and stems
  chopped
50g chopped almonds
1 lemon, half sliced, half
  cut into wedges
2 whole trout (each about
  350–400g), gutted
extra-virgin olive oil, for
  drizzling
sea salt and freshly ground
  black pepper

Preheat the oven to 220°C/200°C fan/Gas 7.

First, make the stuffing. Melt the butter in a pan over a low heat. Add the onion and garlic and sauté for about 5–10 minutes, until soft but not coloured. Then, remove the pan from the heat and set aside.

Tip the breadcrumbs, herbs and almonds into a bowl and season with salt and pepper. Add the onion and garlic mixture and mix well to combine. Taste for seasoning and season again if necessary.

Place a couple of slices of lemon in the belly of each fish, then carefully spoon equal amounts of the stuffing into each belly, spreading it out in an even layer.

Line a large oven tray with baking paper. Season both sides of each trout with salt and pepper, drizzle both sides with olive oil and place both fish side by side in the oven tray. Drizzle again with oil.

Bake the trout for 15 minutes, until a skewer goes easily through the thickest part of each fish.

Allow the fish to rest for 5 minutes, then serve them whole, with wedges of lemon for squeezing over, and a crisp green salad and buttered new potatoes.

Whole Baked Turbot and Boiled Potatoes

Turbot is an amazing fish but it is also an expensive fish. It comes in many sizes so ask your fishmonger for one that suits the occasion. And if all the turbot on offer are too big then ask the fishmonger to slice one right down the middle to get the amount you want.

   We cooked this when we had Phil Howard and Bruce Poole for dinner, and everyone loved it. It's a great show stopper if you're trying to impress. There are a couple of things to remember, first make sure your oven is big enough and then that someone is happy to fillet the fish once cooked.

Serves 4

125g salted butter, softened, plus an extra 15g for the potatoes
1 whole turbot (1–2kg), descaled and well-seasoned with sea salt
150ml dry white wine
400g Desirée potatoes, peeled and cut into about 3cm dice
a handful of flat-leaf parsley, leaves and stems finely chopped
freshly ground white pepper

Heat the oven to 180°C/160°C fan/Gas 4.

Liberally butter a baking tray with half the butter. Place the turbot on top, dark skin facing upwards, then rub the remaining butter over the top and pour over the wine.

Bake the fish for 25–30 minutes, basting it with the liquid in the tray once or twice during cooking, until a skewer inserted at the thickest part of the bone comes out feeling warm when you touch it to your lips. Rest the fish for 25–30 minutes, covered with foil, to allow it to finish cooking and to relax gently.

Meanwhile, cook the potatoes in boiling salted water, until nicely tender, then drain. Season with pepper and half the parsley. Stir through the knob of butter.

Pour the cooking juices from the fish into a sauce jug, stir in the remaining parsley and season with white pepper.

Serve the whole fish at the table in front of your guests, with the boiled potatoes and the sauce.

Pasta and Rice

Asparagus Risotto

There's really no need to over-complicate this simple dish. The secret to success is lots of Parmesan and lots of black pepper. I always use green asparagus for this as I don't think white has such a good flavour but I know there are white asparagus fans out there who will disagree. Don't be stingy with the asparagus!

Use any leftover risotto for arancini – cook the risotto again until thick and gelatinous, then roll it into balls, coat it in breadcrumbs and deep-fry until golden.

Serves 6 as a starter
or 4 as a main

75g unsalted butter, cubed and chilled
2 tablespoons olive oil
1 banana shallot, finely chopped
1 garlic clove, finely chopped
300g carnaroli risotto rice
200ml dry white wine
1 litre hot vegetable stock
a bunch of asparagus, woody ends discarded, stems chopped into rounds, tops whole
75g Parmesan, finely grated
a handful of flat-leaf parsley, leaves and stems chopped, to serve
salt and freshly ground pepper

Heat 20g of the butter and all the oil in a large pan over a low heat. Add the shallot and garlic, season with salt and pepper and fry for about 7–10 minutes, until the shallot is soft but not coloured.

Add the rice, season again, and add another 20g of butter, stirring the rice to toast it, for 3–4 minutes. Add the wine and cook for about 2–3 minutes to evaporate the alcohol. Gradually add the hot stock, a ladleful at a time, stirring continuously and allowing the rice to absorb each addition before pouring in the next. Do not let the rice swim in the stock.

After 14 minutes of adding and stirring, add the asparagus and cook, stirring, for a further 4 minutes, until the rice is al dente – the risotto should be pourable but firm and creamy enough to hold itself together. If it's too thick, add a little more stock.

Remove the pan from the heat and add the remaining butter and the Parmesan, stirring them through the risotto to emulsify and give the risotto a creamy consistency. Check the seasoning and finish with the parsley. Serve immediately.

Courgette and Ogleshield Rigatoni

The secret to this great recipe is to cook the courgettes until they're soft but not mushy. The courgettes will give off water as they cook but you may need to add a little bit extra to stop them from burning.

The Somerset Ogleshield cheese from the Montgomery family is a great addition and a nice change from Parmesan. It's made with unpasteurised milk from Jersey cattle, melts beautifully and is really delicious.

Serves 4

2 courgettes (preferably grezzina), halved lengthways
olive oil
1 garlic clove
½ teaspoon chilli flakes
350g dried rigatoni
a handful of flat-leaf parsley, leaves and stems finely chopped
50g Ogleshield or raclette cheese, grated
50g Parmesan, finely grated
freshly ground black pepper

Cut the courgette halves into half-moon chunks.

Heat a good glug of olive oil in a large pan over a medium heat. Add the courgettes, season with black pepper, and gently sauté for 3–4 minutes, until lightly golden. Add the garlic and chilli flakes and 3 tablespoons of water. Cover the pan with a lid and cook the courgettes for 5 minutes, until they are nicely soft, but not mushy.

Meanwhile, bring a pan of salted water to the boil. Add the rigatoni and cook according to the packet instructions, until al dente.

Drain the cooked pasta, reserving a ladleful or so of the pasta cooking water, and toss the pasta into the cooked courgettes. Stir through the parsley and grated cheeses, and the pasta cooking water to loosen the sauce if needed. Season with an extra twist of black pepper and serve.

Sunday Night Cupboard Spaghetti

This makes a brilliantly quick supper using store cupboard essentials. You just need spaghetti, a tin of tomatoes, garlic and some chilli flakes. Out of all the pasta we eat at home, and we eat a fair amount, this is our go-to recipe and it's always a winner. If you have some bacon or pancetta that needs using, you can add that in with the onion.

Serves 4

olive oil
1 small onion, finely chopped
4 garlic cloves, finely chopped
4 dried peperoncino, broken up, or ½ teaspoon dried chilli flakes
1 x 400g tin of chopped San Marzano tomatoes
370g dried spaghettini
herbs of choice, chopped, to serve (I like flat-leaf parsley and basil)
finely grated Parmesan, to serve

Add a good glug of oil to a frying pan and place the pan over a medium heat. When hot, add the onion and garlic and sauté for a good 10 minutes, until they are really soft but not coloured. Add the dried chilli and the tomatoes and cook for 40 minutes, until you have a thick sauce.

Bring a pan of salted water to the boil. Add the spaghettini and cook according to the packet instructions, until al dente.

Drain the pasta, reserving a few ladlefuls of the cooking water, and add the pasta to the pan with the tomato sauce. Loosen with a little cooking water, if necessary. Stir through your herbs and finish with grated Pparmesan. Serve immediately.

Potato Gnocchi, Wild Garlic and Morels

Few people seem to make gnocchi from scratch but actually it's easier than you think, especially if you have a ricer. And it's well worth the relatively little effort involved. You could use chanterelles or ceps here in place of the morels, and if fresh wild mushrooms are in short supply, then use dried porcini rather than substitute with a farmed variety.

Serves 4

4 Desirée potatoes, washed but left whole and unpeeled
200g type '00' pasta flour
150g Parmesan, finely grated, plus extra to finish
1 egg, beaten
a pinch of freshly grated nutmeg
1 tablespoon olive oil
15g salted butter, plus extra for the wild garlic
200g morel mushrooms, sliced
about 150g wild garlic or spinach
a handful of flat-leaf parsley, leaves picked and finely chopped
sea salt and freshly ground black pepper

Preheat the oven to 200°C/180°C fan/Gas 6.

Place the potatoes on a baking tray and bake for about 1 hour, until tender all the way through, like a perfect jacket potato. Remove them from the oven and, when cool enough to handle, slice them in half and, using a spoon, scoop out the flesh, pressing it through a potato ricer on to a large, floured board or work surface.

Allow the potato to cool for 5 minutes, then add the flour, Parmesan, egg and nutmeg. Season with salt and pepper and, using a pastry scraper, mix the gnocchi mixture, chopping it together to combine until it forms a dough. Knead it gently to bring it into a ball.

Bring a pan of salted water to the boil. Take a small teaspoonful of the gnocchi mixture and drop it into the water. When it floats to the surface, leave it for a minute or so and then scoop it out and taste it for seasoning and texture. Adjust the seasoning of the mixture if necessary and test again. Remove the pan of water from the heat.

When you're happy with the seasoning, divide the mixture into quarters, then halve each quarter so that you have 8 equal portions. Roll each portion into a long sausage with the diameter of a 20-pence piece.

Cut the sausage-shapes along their length into 2cm pieces, then gently roll each piece into gnocchi and place the shaped gnocchi onto a semolina-floured tray or gnocchi board to prevent sticking (aim for about 60 gnocchi altogether). Transfer the trays of gnocchi to the fridge and leave, uncovered, until you're ready to cook.

To cook, bring a pan of salted water to the boil. While the water is heating up, add the olive oil and the butter to a frying pan over a medium heat. When the butter is melted and bubbling, add the morels and sauté for 3–4 minutes, stirring and tossing occasionally, until cooked. Season with salt and pepper. Add an extra knob of butter to the pan and add the wild garlic or spinach. Allow the leaves to wilt for a few seconds.

Add the gnocchi into the boiling water (you'll need about 15 pieces per person) and bring the water back to the boil. When the gnocchi float to the surface, they are cooked. Scoop them out using a slotted spoon and add them to the frying pan with the morels and wild garlic, tossing gently to coat in the buttery sauce.

Add the extra Parmesan, to taste, and the parsley. Check the seasoning and serve in bowls.

Spaghetti Carbonara

Don't mess around with this classic pasta dish. Nothing else is needed to make it perfect; it's like pineapple on pizza – you just don't do it. If you can't source guanciale then use a good-quality pancetta.

Serves 4

20g salted butter
100g diced guanciale or pancetta
2 garlic cloves, finely chopped
a pinch of dried chilli
370g dried spaghetti
3 large eggs, well beaten
50g pecorino, Romano or Parmesan, finely grated, plus extra to serve
freshly ground black pepper, to serve

Heat a large frying pan or sauté pan over a medium heat (the pan needs to be big enough to hold the spaghetti when it's cooked). Add the butter and leave it to melt, then add the guanciale or pancetta and leave it to cook and crisp up – about 5 minutes.

Add the garlic and chilli, and sauté for a further 1 minute, then remove the pan from the heat.

Add the spaghetti to a large pan of salted boiling water and cook it according to the packet instructions, until al dente.

Just before you drain the spaghetti, reheat the pancetta or guanciale mixture over a low heat. When the pasta is ready, drain it and add it to the large pan with the guanciale or pancetta mixture. Add the eggs and the cheese and stir through. Serve immediately – the eggs should still be runny and not fully cooked.

Serve with extra cheese for sprinkling over and a pepper mill of freshly ground black pepper for your guests to help themselves.

Sausage and Pea Risotto

For me, a risotto is a gentle labour of love and I think you need to do all the stirring and put in all the time. If you do then you will be well rewarded.

You will need to get a really great sausage for this dish. You can buy some brilliant British-made spicy Italian sausages with fennel and chilli – just crumble them in to the rice. Either carnaroli or arborio rice work really well for this recipe and you could use broad beans or leeks instead of the peas.

Serves 6 as a starter
or 4 as a main

75g salted butter
extra-virgin olive oil
2 garlic cloves, finely
    chopped
1 small onion or 1 banana
    shallot, finely chopped
300g carnaroli risotto rice
200ml dry white wine
4 spicy fennel Italian
    sausages, skins
    discarded, meat
    crumbled
1 litre hot chicken stock
100g fresh or frozen peas
75g Parmesan, finely
    grated
sea salt and freshly ground
    black pepper

Heat 20g of the butter and a glug of olive oil in a large pan over a medium heat. Add the garlic and onion, season with salt and pepper and fry for about 10 minutes, until the onion is transparent but not coloured.

Add the rice, season again, and add the remaining butter, stirring the rice to toast it for about 3–4 minutes. Add the wine and cook for about 2–3 minutes to evaporate the alcohol. Add the crumbled sausagemeat and cook for 2 minutes, then gradually add the hot stock, a ladleful at a time, stirring continuously, and allowing the rice to absorb each addition before pouring in the next. Do not let the rice swirl or swim in the stock.

After about 14 minutes of adding and stirring, add the peas (or at 16 minutes if they're frozen) and cook for a further 4–6 minutes, until the rice is al dente – the risotto should be pourable but firm and creamy enough to hold itself together. If it's too thick, add a little more stock.

Remove the pan from the heat, add the Parmesan and check the seasoning, then serve immediately.

Maltagliati Sausage Ragù

The garlic and fennel are perfect flavourings for this classic Italian recipe traditionally made up of the leftover trimmings of fresh pasta. Add a little of the pasta cooking water to give it a bit more of a sauce.

Frozen peas are great to throw in at the end, though radicchio would be equally good.

Serves 4

2 tablespoons olive oil
2 garlic cloves, sliced
½ fennel bulb, finely diced
pinch of fennel seeds,
    toasted and crushed
pinch of coriander seeds,
    toasted and crushed
4 spicy fennel sausages,
    meat squeezed out
175ml white wine
300g fresh maltagliati pasta
1 heaped teaspoon salted
    butter
grated Parmesan, to serve
a handful of flat-leaf
    parsley, leaves picked
    and chopped, to serve

Add the olive oil to a large frying pan over a low heat. Add the garlic and fennel and crushed spices and sauté for 10 minutes, until soft but without any colour.

Using your hands, break up the sausagemeat and add it to the pan. Stir and allow the meat to colour and lose its rawness.

Add the wine and deglaze the pan, scraping up the goodness on the bottom, then let it bubble away until it's reduced by about half. Add a couple of tablespoons of water and cook for 10 minutes to form a sauce.

In the meantime, cook the pasta in boiling salted water according to the packet instructions, until al dente. Drain and immediately toss the pasta into the pan with the sausagemeat. Add the butter and allow it to melt and glaze the pasta, then finish with a sprinkling of Parmesan and flat-leaf parsley, to serve.

Pappardelle with Ischian Rabbit Sauce

This is a dish I learnt from a chef called Alfonso at Ristorante Montecorvo when I was cooking at an event on the beautiful Italian volcanic island of Ischia. Alfonso was full of personality and a lovely man. I remember the pure simplicity of how he cooked the sauce and how delicious it was. As always, it's all about using the best ingredients you can find – so top-quality ripe tomatoes, fresh garlic and freshly snipped herbs.

You could also mash in the livers from the rabbit towards the end of cooking just to bring an extra richness to the sauce – ask your butcher for them when he's jointing the rabbit.

Serves 4

50ml extra-virgin olive oil
3 whole rabbit legs, boned and diced
2 garlic cloves, finely chopped
1 teaspoon tomato purée
10 very ripe cherry tomatoes
250ml dry white wine
500g fresh pappardelle
a handful of flat-leaf parsley, leaves and stems chopped
a handful of marjoram, leaves picked and chopped
freshly grated Parmesan, to serve
sea salt and freshly ground black pepper

Heat the olive oil in a pan over a medium heat. Add the diced rabbit and sauté for 3–4 minutes, until the meat has taken on some colour. Add the garlic, tomato purée and cherry tomatoes, season with salt and pepper, and cook for about 5 minutes, or until the tomatoes start to break down.

Add the wine to the pan, along with 1 glass of water and bring the liquid to the boil. Lower the heat to a simmer and cook for 40 minutes, until you have a nice, thick sauce.

Cook the pappardelle in a pan of boiling salted water, until just al dente (about 2–3 minutes, or according to the packet instructions), then drain.

Immediately add the flat-leaf parsley and marjoram to the sauce, then add the pasta and toss to coat the ribbons. Serve immediately with freshly grated Parmesan.

Vegetables

Roasted Italian Peppers

Ideally, when in season, you should use long Italian peppers from Carmagnola for this recipe, but definitely not Dutch or bell peppers which lack flavour. There's a great producer on the Isle of Wight who supplies some excellent Romano peppers which we use at Lime Wood and Murano. They're so tender we don't need to peel them.

My friend Jayne lives in Torino and when the peppers are in season, her mother-in-law cooks them, adds salsa verde and anchovies, and then freezes them, ready to be enjoyed all the year round when friends visit.

Serves 4

2 large Italian red peppers
2 tablespoons sherry
　　vinegar
8 anchovy fillets, drained,
　　oil reserved
1 rosemary sprig
1 thyme sprig
1 garlic clove, bashed
extra-virgin olive oil
10 basil leaves, torn
sea salt

Either by heating your oven as hot as it will go, or over an open gas flame, scorch the peppers until the skins are brown and blackened in places, but not burnt, and the peppers are three-quarters cooked.

Place them in a bowl and sprinkle them liberally with the sherry vinegar, sea salt and anchovy oil. Pop in the rosemary and thyme sprigs and the garlic, cover the bowl with a plate and leave to steam in the residual heat for 30 minutes, until the peppers are fully cooked through.

Slide off the blackened skins from the peppers and remove the seeds. Tear the peppers into 6 or 8 pieces, depending on size, then strain the juices into a bowl. Stir in just enough olive oil to make a dressing. Discard the herbs and garlic.

Arrange the pepper pieces on a serving dish and scatter over the anchovies and torn basil leaves. Spoon over the dressing and serve.

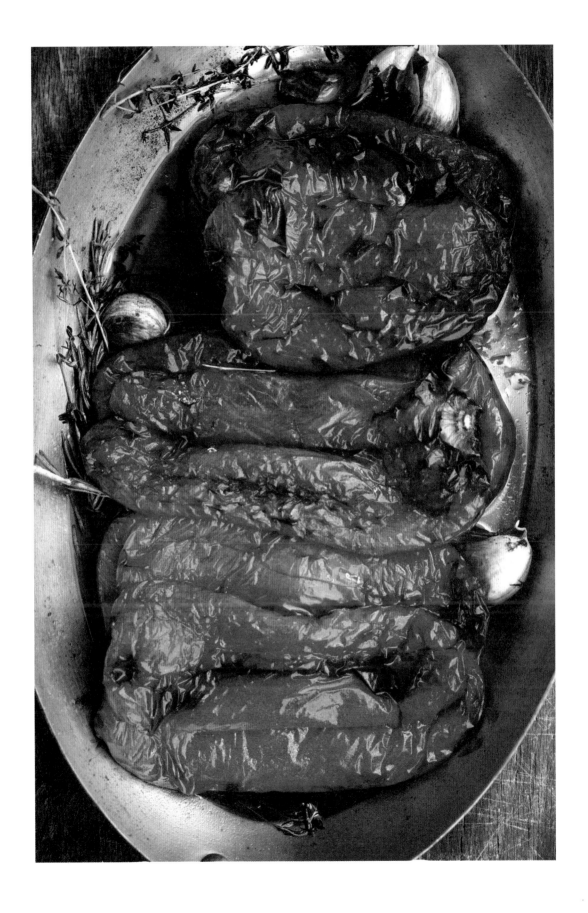

Baked Violet Aubergines with Orange and Mint

This is Neil's recipe. The aubergines are slow-baked and then smothered with orange and mint to finish. They are lovely and soft and not at all oily, unlike some aubergine dishes. You could also add chilli, coriander or Japanese mirin. The best aubergines are Italian ones – you can't beat them when they're in season.

**Serves 4 generously
as a starter**

juice of 4 oranges and
    zest of 2
2 violet aubergines
200ml extra-virgin olive oil
2 mint sprigs, leaves picked
    and roughly chopped
sea salt and freshly ground
    black pepper

First, pour the orange juice (make sure you've zested 2 of the oranges first!) into a small saucepan and place it over a medium heat. Allow the juice to come to a gentle simmer and bubble away until it is reduced by half. Set aside and leave to cool completely.

Meanwhile, preheat the oven to 180°C/160°C fan/Gas 4.

Wrap the aubergines in foil, place them in a baking tray and bake them for 40–50 minutes, until just tender at the part nearest the stalk. Remove the aubergines from the oven and leave them in the tray just as they are for at least 20 minutes (they'll finish cooking in this time), then unwrap them and gently peel off the skin.

Depending on their size, cut each aubergine into 10–12 wedges while they're still warm. Arrange the wedges on a suitable serving platter and season liberally with sea salt.

Combine the reduced orange juice with all the orange zest and olive oil in a small bowl to create a dressing and drizzle this liberally over the seasoned aubergine slices. Finish with a scattering of chopped mint and some freshly ground black pepper. Serve immediately.

Braised Courgettes

When courgettes are in season, they're one of my favourite vegetables; they're easy to cook and are very simple to prepare. I like to use the Italian Romano courgettes; they're striped on the outside and packed full of flavour inside. Courgettes can take some big flavoured herbs so you could use lovage or marjoram in place of the parsley.

Serves 4–6

100ml olive oil
3 garlic cloves, bashed
6 dried peperoncino, lightly crushed, or ½–1 teaspoon chilli flakes
6 courgettes (preferably grezzina or romano), cut into rough, bite-sized chunks
a handful of flat-leaf parsley, leaves and stems finely chopped, to serve
sea salt

Heat the olive oil in a large, deep, frying pan over a medium heat. Add the garlic and crushed chillies and cook for 1 minute, until they sizzle but don't take on any colour.

Add the courgettes, season with a little sea salt, and add 4 tablespoons of water. Cover the pan with a tight-fitting lid, then turn the heat down to low and cook the courgettes for 20–30 minutes, until nicely tender when pierced with a knife or the tip of a spoon. While the courgettes are cooking, remove the lid to stir them occasionally and add a touch of water if they start to dry out. If they take on a bit of colour that's no problem, the important thing is that they are nicely cooked and tender.

Check the seasoning and add the chopped parsley before serving.

Tardive and Castelfranco Salad

This is a dish that we put on the menu when we opened Café Murano in Bermondsey. Its roots are in Venice and I love it. My grandmother would always serve us radicchio, very finely sliced, and since then I've always loved bitter leaves.

Castelfranco radicchio is less tart than tardive and the lovely flavours of the lemon zest and the pecorino help to cut through the bitterness and add a touch of sweetness. The key to success is to use tons of good pecorino, though Winchester Gold or a young Montgomery Cheddar would be good alternatives.

Serves 2 as a starter
or 4 as a side

1 tardive radicchio, washed well and dried
1 castelfranco, washed well and dried
finely grated zest of 1 unwaxed lemon
50g pecorino, shaved
extra-virgin olive oil
sea salt

Place the salad leaves, lemon zest and cheese in a large bowl. Toss well and finish with olive oil and a sprinkling of sea salt. Serve immediately.

Chicory, Blue Cheese and Grape Salad

This is quite a 70s salad, and came about when Neil and I were guests of the brilliant chef Phil Howard at his house in the French Alps. At one meal he served a salad similar to this and it was just delicious, so I recreated it when we got home.

Chicory is one of my favourite ingredients, and I use the whole leaves for this recipe. I like to use normal red grapes but you could use Muscatels when they're in season in September – they'd pair really well with a strong blue like Stichelton or Roquefort. You could also serve this with a classic salad dressing or a bit of orange dressing, and feel free to add walnuts.

Serves 4 as a starter

4 yellow chicory
3 tablespoons extra-virgin olive oil
1 tablespoon white wine vinegar
½ teaspoon Dijon mustard
100g seedless red grapes, halved
100g gorgonzola or another blue cheese, crumbled
2 pickled walnuts, chopped
sea salt and freshly ground black pepper

Using a small knife, remove the chicory root and cut the chicory down the middle. Gently remove the leaves, trying to keep them as whole as possible.

Mix the olive oil and vinegar in a bowl, add the mustard and season sparingly with salt and pepper.

Arrange the chicory leaves on a large platter and scatter over the grapes and cheese. Finish with the chopped pickled walnuts and pour over the dressing. Serve immediately.

Asian Slaw

The spices, limes and jalapeño peppers are integral to this simple slaw with a kick. It's a great accompaniment to simple grilled chicken or fish and just delicious served with bread.

It's always best if this has a couple of hours to marinate so the raw vegetables can absorb the dressing flavours. If you leave out the coriander and mint you can prep this slaw a day in advance – add the herbs when you're ready to serve.

Serves 8 as a side

300g white cabbage, finely sliced
150g mangetouts, finely sliced
1 jalapeño pepper, finely sliced
1 small red onion, finely sliced
2 Granny Smith apples, cored and finely sliced
4 tablespoons sesame oil
2 tablespoons light soy sauce
juice and finely grated zest of 2 limes
a handful of mint, leaves picked and roughly chopped
a handful of coriander, leaves picked and roughly chopped
1 teaspoon sesame seeds, toasted
1 teaspoon poppy seeds, toasted
sea salt

Tip the cabbage, mangetouts, jalapeño, onion and apples into a large bowl and use your hands to combine. Add the oil, soy sauce, lime juice and zest and season with salt. Mix well and leave to stand for at least 15 minutes, but ideally a few hours, then add the herbs and mix again. Sprinkle with the toasted seeds, then serve.

Forgotten Carrots

This dish comes from Neil's time in France working for Michel Bras in Aubrac. This simple recipe calls for the best carrots you can find, a good amount of butter and some delicious spices. Removing the water content concentrates all the natural sugars, giving you lovely, sweet, juicy carrots.

These pair really well with a roasted pork dish – just delicious.

Serves 4 as a side

1 bunch of large organic carrots, tops attached (the size is very important)
100ml pomace oil or a neutral oil, such as sunflower or vegetable
100g unsalted butter
2 star anise
2 black cardamom pods
sea salt, to taste

Trim the carrots, leaving a little of the green tops attached, then wash them thoroughly to remove any dirt. Drain them in a colander.

Preheat the oven to 160°C/140°C fan/Gas 2–3.

Heat the pomace or other neutral oil in a large saucepan over a medium heat (the pan needs to be large enough to fit the carrots in a single layer, otherwise do this in batches). When the oil is hot, add the carrots. Cook them in the pan, turning frequently, until caramelised all over – about 8–10 minutes.

When the carrots are evenly coloured, add the butter and the whole spices, and season with salt. Allow the butter to foam, then transfer the carrots to a roasting dish, place them in the oven and forget about them for 40 minutes–1 hour, depending on their size, until they are crinkly on the outside but soft and juicy in the middle. Discard the star anise and cardamom pods before you serve.

Globe Artichokes

I just love artichokes and this is one of the best dishes ever. Some people can be put off by the prep that's needed, but actually this is a simple recipe with minimum prep. You just need to cut the root off, boil the artichokes and peel them down. They're sometimes messy to eat but are great things to share with friends, everyone tearing off leaves and dipping them in the anchovy mayonnaise and sucking out the soft and tastiest parts of the petal.

The anchovy mayonnaise clings to the leaves (see page 46) which I prefer to the traditional accompaniment of a liquidy vinaigrette.

Serves 6

6 globe artichokes
2 thyme sprigs
$\frac{1}{2}$ lemon
4 garlic cloves
1 star anise
anchovy mayonnaise
(see page 46), to serve
sea salt

Snap the stalk off the base of each artichoke and discard. Place the artichokes in a large pan – big enough to hold all of them. Add the thyme sprigs, lemon half, garlic cloves and star anise and season with salt. Cover with cold water and top with a plate to keep the artichokes beneath the surface of the water as they cook.

Place the pan over a high heat and bring the water to the boil, then reduce the heat to a simmer and cook the artichokes for 30 minutes, until the bottom of the artichokes yield to the point of a knife. Remove the pan from the heat, allow the artichokes to cool in the water, then drain them well, making sure they drain upside down to remove any excess water caught inside. Serve whole with the anchovy mayonnaise.

Curried Cauliflower, Pine Nuts and Raisins

Cauliflower is so versatile; it can take spice and can handle heat. I use whatever curry powder we have in the cupboard for this dish. It's Sicilian-inspired, using pine nuts and raisins, and you could use almonds or walnuts instead as they'd both work really well. This recipe is great for using up stuff from the larder; don't be afraid to substitute other dried fruits or experiment with spices.

Serves 4 as a starter

1 large head of cauliflower, leaves discarded, florets and stalk cut into chunky pieces
2–3 teaspoons curry powder or garam masala
olive oil
50g salted butter
2 teaspoons coriander seeds
50g raisins
20g capers
juice of 1 lemon
a handful of lovage or coriander, leaves and stalks chopped
50g pine nuts, lightly toasted
sea salt and freshly ground black pepper

Heat the oven to 180°C/160°C fan/Gas 4.

Mix the cauliflower pieces in a bowl with the curry powder or garam masala, according to taste. Season with salt.

Pour a liberal amount of olive oil into an ovenproof pan and heat it over a medium heat. When the oil is hot, add the seasoned cauliflower and cook for 5 minutes, until lightly golden and caramelised. Add the butter and continue to cook for 3 minutes, until the butter foams.

Add the coriander seeds, raisins, capers and lemon juice, stir to combine, then transfer the cauliflower mixture to an ovenproof dish and roast it for 30 minutes, until the cauliflower is nicely tender.

Remove the dish from the oven and allow the cauliflower to cool to room temperature, then stir in the chopped herbs and the toasted pine nuts. Check for seasoning and serve.

Turnip and Celeriac Gratin

I love turnips; I think they are under-used but are so delicious. I made this years ago at The Connaught as a change from a traditional potato dauphinoise. The key to success is to cut the thinnest slices possible. It's a dish to serve with roasted lamb or a ham (see pages 80 or 180) and is brilliant with a roasted joint of beef; a great winter dish.

Serves 6 as a side

2 large turnips (about 300g), peeled, then very thinly sliced
1 celeriac (about 600g; or ½ large one), peeled, then very thinly sliced
200ml double cream
1 garlic clove, finely chopped
1 rosemary sprig, leaves picked and finely chopped
50g salted butter, plus extra for greasing
sea salt and freshly ground black pepper

Preheat the oven to 200°C/180°C fan/Gas 6.

Place the turnip and celeriac slices in a large bowl. Season with salt and pepper and add the cream, garlic and rosemary. Mix well.

Lightly grease a 30cm x 20cm baking dish with butter. Tip the contents of the bowl into the dish and press down. Dot the 50g of butter over the top and bake for 40 minutes, until the vegetables are tender (you should be able to insert a knife easily through the layers) and golden brown, and the cream has thickened. Serve immediately. (It's delicious with roasted lamb, but good by itself, too.)

Baked Vacherin Cheese

This is quite fancy fare and a dish we serve at Murano in Mayfair. It's also a dish that we've served at home at dinner parties. Use white truffle if you're feeling really decadent or you're out to impress. But if you don't have white truffle then use black truffle or leave the truffle out – it will be different but equally as delicious.

You must bake the vacherin until it's really soft on top – no need to do anything else with it. If you can't get vacherin then a good, ripe Camembert would work.

Serves 6

750ml olive oil
1 rosemary sprig
10 new potatoes or small
    Ratte potatoes
1 x 450g vacherin cheese
1 white truffle
sea salt

First, prepare the potatoes – you can make them ahead and then reheat them in the oven with the vacherin, if you like. Pour the olive oil into a small pan big enough to hold the potatoes tightly. Add the rosemary and season with sea salt. Add the potatoes and place the pan over a medium heat. Bring the oil to the boil, then immediately reduce the heat to a low simmer and confit the potatoes for about 25–30 minutes, until tender (the length of time will depend on the size of your potatoes). Using a slotted spoon, remove the potatoes from the oil and leave them to cool before cutting them in half lengthways. (Strain the oil to use it again another time.)

Heat the oven to 220°C/200°C fan/Gas 7.

Place the vacherin, in its box or tight-fitting oven-proof dish, on a baking tray and bake it in the oven for 15–25 minutes, until it starts to soften. How long the cheese takes precisely will depend on the size of the cheese – it's ready when it feels soft and wobbly when you remove the lid and touch the top.

Carefully remove the lid, spoon over the confit potatoes, slice the white truffle and sprinkle the slices on top. Serve immediately.

Oven-roasted Potatoes

I grew up eating this dish of very small roast potatoes, essentially the Italian classic *patate al forno*. Roasted potatoes need to be brilliant. And the secret to brilliance is good oil, flavours of garlic and rosemary, a good amount of sea salt, potatoes diced small with the skin on then thrown into a big pan to roast in the oven.

If you don't have a flameproof oven dish, you can heat the oil in a roasting tin in the oven, then add the potatoes, garlic and rosemary and continue as in the method.

Serves 6

100ml olive oil
4 large potatoes, unpeeled
   and cut into 2cm dice
2 garlic cloves, crushed
1 rosemary sprig, leaves
   picked and finely
   chopped
a handful of flat-leaf
   parsley, leaves picked
   and finely chopped
sea salt

Heat the oven to 220°C/200°C fan/Gas 7.

Heat the oil in a large, ovenproof frying pan or heavy-duty sauté pan over a medium heat. When hot, add the potatoes and throw in the crushed garlic and the rosemary. Give everything a stir, then transfer the potatoes to the oven to roast for 10 minutes. Remove the pan from the oven, shake the potatoes to turn them so that they roast evenly, then return them to the oven.

Roast the potatoes for a further 20–30 minutes, until crispy and golden. Remove the dish from the oven and drain away any excess oil. Tip the potatoes into a warmed serving dish, sprinkle over the parsley and season with salt. Serve immediately.

Slow-cooked Onions

These onions are a great accompaniment to so many dishes, especially chicken or beef. They can also be served with bread to mop up all the delicious sweet oniony juices.

I believe that onions should be cooked low and slow in order to get the best out of them. Roscoff in season are the absolute best for this, though small white onions or long banana shallots work really well too – just keep the skins on. It's a classic French preparation and so easy to do at home. The onions are very forgiving when cooked this way. You could also just lightly colour them on the hob first and then transfer to the oven, or if you have an Aga, you could simply pop them in the slow oven and leave alone for a few hours to cook to perfection.

Serves 4

5 Roscoff onions or small white onions
1 tablespoon olive oil
25g salted butter
3 thyme sprigs
sea salt and freshly ground black pepper

Halve the onions across their middles (skins on).

Over a medium heat, heat the olive oil and butter together in a frying pan or saucepan large enough to hold the onions in a single layer. When the butter has melted and starts to bubble, season the onions with salt and pepper and add them to the pan cut-side downwards. Allow them to sizzle for 3–4 minutes, until golden brown, then turn them over so that they are skin-side downwards.

Add the thyme and 5 tablespoons of water and cover the surface with a piece of baking paper or put the lid on the pan. Turn the heat down to low and cook for 10–15 minutes, removing the covering to turn occasionally and adding a little more butter and water as necessary, until the onions are soft enough that a knife pierces them easily.

Serve the onions in their skins – they are delicious with any roasted meat.

Neighbours

Pat and Ben's Aubergines

This is a recipe dedicated to Pat and Ben. They moved into a house around the corner from us in Spitalfields and, as we were old friends, we said we'd throw a large party to welcome them to the neighbourhood. I said I'd do the food and Pat said she'd bring the wine. When she dropped off the booze at about 1pm on the afternoon of the party she freaked out that nothing at all had been prepared. Seeing her shock, Neil and I swiftly made a move to the kitchen and much to her surprise and relief pulled it all together just in time. I cooked everything for the party except for Pat's aubergine dish that Neil made. He grilled them simply with yoghurt, oil and lemon. And everyone at the party – and I mean everyone – kept talking about the sodding aubergines and not a word was said about any of my many delicious dishes!

The aubergines work really well on a barbecue or a ridged grill pan, giving you lovely char marks and blisterings. And as I know very well from Pat's welcoming party, they are perfect for entertaining.

Serves 4

2 violet aubergines (the round ones), sliced crossways into 2mm-thick slices
olive oil, for drizzling
300g thick-set Greek yoghurt
2 garlic cloves, grated
20g fresh ginger, peeled and grated
juice and zest of 1 lemon
a large handful of coriander, chopped
a small handful of mint leaves, chopped, plus extra to serve
sea salt

Drizzle the aubergine slices with olive oil and season generously with salt. Heat a chargrill pan or barbecue to hot and add the aubergine slices to the grill. Cook until nicely charred and tender.

While the aubergines are cooking, mix together the other ingredients to make the dressing. Check the seasoning and set aside.

Once the aubergines are ready, remove them from the grill to a serving dish. Smother them in the dressing and serve sprinkled with extra mint leaves.

Stevie G's Puttanesca

Stevie G makes a great puttanesca, perfect for a relaxed supper. This is his recipe. The beauty of his sauce is that you can adapt it to make it work for you – splash in some red wine for added finesse, or make it spicier with added peperoncino, richer with more black olives, or more acid with added capers (more is always more in this case). Stevie serves his puttanesca with penne pasta, but truth be told spaghetti is probably best (and certainly more usual). We have to forgive him, though – he has good reason for straying from tradition, owing to what he calls his pasta-PTSD. Having been given spaghetti at dinner with a girlfriend's very posh parents, Stevie found he had to wipe pasta sauce off his glasses. His dignity was in tatters and they split up soon afterwards. Henceforth he uses penne to avoid tears at dinnertime.

Serves 4 (or 2 very hungry people)

olive oil
3 garlic cloves, finely chopped
2 x 400g tins of good-quality chopped tomatoes
2 tablespoons good-quality anchovies, drained
2 teaspoons drained capers
2 tablespoons pitted and roughly chopped black olives
1 teaspoon caster sugar
a good pinch of crumbled dried peperoncino
a good grinding of black pepper
350g dried penne or spaghetti
good-quality finely grated Parmesan, to serve

Pour a little olive oil into a large pan over a low heat. When hot, add the garlic and fry for about 1 minute, until soft and translucent, but not coloured and definitely not burnt (which would ruin the flavour of the sauce). Add the tomatoes, then the anchovies, capers, olives, sugar, peperoncino and pepper. Bring the sauce to a gentle simmer and leave it to simmer away for at least 45 minutes without a lid over a really gentle heat, until it has reduced to a lovely, thick consistency that will stick to the pasta.

Towards the end of the sauce cooking time, bring a pan of well-salted water to the boil and cook the pasta until al dente, according to the packet instructions. Drain and transfer the pasta to the sauce, stirring to coat. Scoop the pasta and sauce into warmed bowls and serve it with best-quality Parmesan for sprinkling over.

Nick's Lamb Curry

Nick and his wife Kate are great friends, and their youngest son, George, is our godson. Nick makes a great curry and they often brings us 'leftovers'. And not a tupperware of just the curry, but the rice, the raita, the garnish – the whole shebang and it's delicious. This curry is made from lamb shoulder and is full of spice. It's not oily, which lamb often is, and has the most wonderful flavours.

Serves 6

6 tablespoons vegetable oil
1 cinnamon stick
5 green cardamom pods, cracked
1 black cardamom pod, cracked
10 curry leaves
2 bay leaves
2 tablespoons fennel seeds
3 onions, chopped
3 tomatoes, chopped
3 tablespoons coriander seeds
1 tablespoon white poppy seeds
½ teaspoon ground turmeric
2 tablespoons extra-hot chilli powder
1 teaspoon salt
8 garlic cloves
5cm piece of fresh ginger, peeled and grated, plus extra to garnish
5 green chillies, deseeded and chopped
1kg diced lamb shoulder
200ml coconut milk
juice of ½ lemon
1 teaspoon *kasuri methi* (dried fenugreek leaves)
coriander, chopped, to garnish

To serve
cooked white rice or warmed flat breads
onion salad
cucumber raita

Pour the oil into a large saucepan and place it over a medium heat. When the oil is hot, add the cinnamon stick, green and black cardamom pods, curry leaves, bay leaves and 1 teaspoon of the fennel seeds. Stir for 1 minute to release the flavours, then add the onions. Cook the spices and onions for 10–12 minutes, until the onions have softened and turned a light brown colour. Add the tomatoes and stir for 5 minutes, until the tomatoes have collapsed.

Meanwhile, put the remaining fennel seeds, along with the coriander seeds and poppy seeds in a spice grinder and grind them to a fine powder. Tip the powder into a bowl and mix in the turmeric, chilli powder and salt. Set aside.

In a mini food processor, whizz the garlic, ginger and chillies with a dash of water to form a paste.

Stir the spice powder and the garlic and ginger paste into the onions and tomatoes in the pan. Fry, stirring for 3–4 minutes to release the flavours, taking care not to let the mixture catch on the bottom of the pan – add a dash of water, if necessary. Add the lamb and fry for 5 minutes, until the meat has browned on all sides.

Add the coconut milk, lemon juice and *kasuri methi*. Stir to combine. Bring the liquid to the boil, then add just enough water to cover the meat. Bring to the boil again, then put a lid on the pan, reduce the heat to low and simmer for 2–3 hours, stirring occasionally and replacing the lid, until the meat is tender. Check the consistency of the sauce 30 minutes before the end of the cooking time – if it looks too runny, remove the lid for the remaining time to give the sauce a chance to thicken.

Garnish with juliennes of ginger and a sprinkling of fresh coriander, and serve with rice or Indian flat breads, an onion salad and a cucumber raita.

Pat's Leg of Lamb

Packed full of garlic and anchovies, Pat Llewellyn's leg of lamb is inspired by Jamie Oliver's, and is a great crowd-pleaser.

Pat's parents owned a B&B in Carmarthen and she grew up in a wonderful environment of entertaining and hospitality and so quickly learned the art of hosting. Pat was a great cook and host and loved to feed others – this was her go-to recipe for a celebration.

Serves 6–8

1 leg of lamb (about 2kg)
a handful of rosemary
    sprigs, roughly torn
10 anchovy fillets
1 lemon, halved
olive oil
250ml white wine
2 garlic bulbs, halved
    horizontally
sea salt and freshly ground
    black pepper

Pre-heat the oven to 220°C/200°C fan/Gas 7.

Remove the lamb from the fridge about an hour before you intend to start cooking – this makes it easier to insert the anchovies and rosemary and allows for a more even roast.

Make about 10 slashes across the flesh of the lamb leg with a small knife, then push the torn sprigs of rosemary and the anchovy fillets into the slashes. Finally, rub the cut sides of the lemon halves over the lamb and season with salt and pepper.

Transfer the lamb to a large, ovenproof dish and drizzle over a couple of tablespoons of olive oil, then pour the white wine all over.

Roast the lamb for 20 minutes, then reduce the oven temperature to 200°C/180°C fan/Gas 6 and roast for a further 40 minutes, turning occasionally (this helps to crisp up the skin). Then, add the garlic bulb halves to the roasting dish so that they cook alongside the lamb. Roast for a further 30 minutes–1 hour, until the meat is cooked through. Remove from the oven, cover the lamb with foil and leave to rest for 15 minutes. Serve in slices with squeezed-out cloves of the roasted garlic on the side.

Basil's Christmas Ham

Basil is one of our neighbours and one of Pat's best mates. He always says to me that food is the enemy, and that he hates to cook, but every other year or so he has a post-Christmas party where his ham is the star of the show, followed by Christmas pudding or mince pies. This is my variation on his recipe.

Serves 15–20

4–5kg piece of unsmoked gammon
2 carrots, halved
1 onion, peeled and quartered
1 leek, chopped into large chunks
1 bay leaf
2 thyme sprigs
2 heaped tablespoons demerara sugar
1 tablespoon English mustard
1 tablespoon wholegrain mustard
turnip and celeriac gratin (see page 162), to serve, (optional)

Place the ham in a large bowl or saucepan, cover with water and soak for up to 8–10 hours. Replace the water at least once during the soaking time. This removes some of the excess salt used to cure it.

When you're ready to cook, drain the ham and transfer it to a clean pan, large enough to hold the ham, with the carrots, onions, leek, bay leaf and thyme. Cover with fresh water, cover with a lid, place the pan over a medium heat and cook the ham for up to 2 hours. The time will depend on the size of your ham – the usual rule of thumb is 20 minutes per 450g. Make sure you keep it topped up with extra water during cooking.

Remove the ham from the stock and then strain the liquid into a jug. Leave the stock to cool, then transfer it to an airtight container and refrigerate it for up to 3 days or freeze it for 1 month – you can use it as stock for soups and risottos. Discard the vegetables and herbs in the sieve.

Allow the ham to cool and remove the skin, but not the fat. Score the fat into a criss-cross pattern to form diamonds all over.

Heat the oven to 200°C/180°C fan/Gas 6.

Mix together the sugar and mustards and use a pastry brush to evenly coat the ham all over. Transfer the ham to a roasting tin and roast it for 30 minutes, until the meat is cooked through, tender and nice and sticky on the outside. Leave to cool before slicing. It's delicious served with the turnip gratin, or gratinated leeks and a parsley sauce.

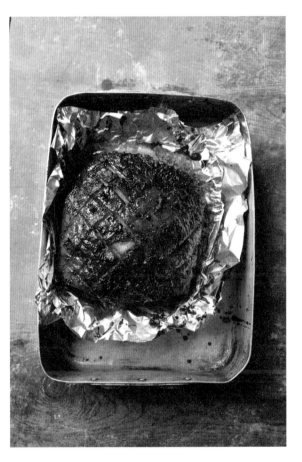

James' Haggis

This book is all about sharing food with friends and family, and for me this recipe is the epitome of that. Neil grew up in central Scotland so of course we celebrate Burns Night every January. And every year James and Neil prepare the haggis to be served with neeps and tatties. We do a very traditional Burns Night, starting with a soup like cock-a-leekie or Cullen skink (see pages 60 and 66) and of course we read the great man's poems when presenting the haggis.

Ox bung is also known as beef or ox caps, and is supplied in 2m x 1m lengths – just ask your butcher.

Serves 6

1 ox bung
warm water, for soaking
1.5kg lamb's pluck (heart, lungs and liver)
1 small onion, quartered
1 celery stick, cut into 4 equal pieces
1 leek, cut into 4 equal pieces
50g lamb fat
3 onions, finely chopped
500g pinhead oats
500g minced beef, lamb trimmings or finely chopped stewing steak
200g fresh lamb or beef suet
1 nutmeg, finely grated
2 teaspoons ground allspice
1 teaspoon ground mace
4 tablespoons sea salt
2 tablespoons freshly ground black pepper

Soak the bung in the warm water overnight to soften.

Tip the lamb pluck into a large saucepan that leaves plenty of room and cover with cold water. Place the pan over a high heat and bring the liquid to the boil. Immediately remove the pan from the heat, drain the lamb's pluck and rinse it under cold running water.

Clean the pan and return the pluck to it. Again cover the pluck with cold water and place it this time over a medium heat. Bring the liquid to a simmer, spoon off and discard the scum that rises to the surface and add the quartered onion, celery and leek. Gently simmer, uncovered, for 2 hours. Remove the pan from the heat, set it aside and leave the liquid and pluck to cool (don't throw away the liquid).

While the pluck is cooking, melt the lamb fat in a frying pan over a low heat. Add the chopped onions and fry very gently for 30 minutes, until really soft and sweet. Tip out the onions on to a plate and set aside to cool.

Clean out the frying pan and wipe it dry. Place it back over a low heat and add the oats. Toast for 3 minutes, stirring frequently and watching carefully so that they don't catch, until they smell nutty.

Once the pluck has cooled, separate out the various parts. Finely chop the lungs and heart on a board and grate the liver using the coarse side of a grater. Tip all the pieces into a bowl and add the meat, suet, oats, spices, salt and pepper. Add the cooked onions and a good splash of the cooking liquid from the pluck (not too much).

Heat a small pan and fry a bit of the mixture over a medium heat until cooked to check the seasoning.

Cut the bung into 6 equal pieces. Divide the mixture into 6 equal portions, and use it to stuff the bung pieces; you want to leave a good amount of room for expansion, so keep each section just two thirds full.

Tie the ends tightly with butcher's string. Bring a large pan of water to the boil over a high heat, then reduce the heat to a simmer. Add the haggis to the water and leave it to simmer for 2 hours, taking care that the water doesn't boil – that would burst the bung.

After 2 hours, remove the haggis from the water and serve it immediately with neeps and tatties.

Alternatively, leave it to cool, then wrap it in foil and refrigerate it for up to 2 days. To reheat, preheat the oven to 200°C/180°C fan/Gas 6. Wrap the haggis in foil, place it in an ovenproof dish and pour over some boiling water. Reheat in the oven for 45 minutes, until piping hot.

Jonathan's Welsh Cakes

I know three people who make wonderful Welsh cakes: my mum, my neighbour Jonathan and Welsh John from St. John's Restaurant. The consistency should be halfway between a scone and a biscuit, and the flavourings are butter, sugar and currants or sultanas, but you could add lemon or orange for a bit of extra zing.

For proper Welsh cakes you need a skillet rather than a frying pan and use only a little bit of butter to cook. The cakes are best plated straight off the skillet served with some really good butter.

Makes about 24

225g self-raising flour
110g unsalted butter, cubed and chilled
55g caster sugar, plus extra for sprinkling
50g sultanas (or a good handful)
1–2 eggs

Sift the flour into a large bowl and, using your fingertips, rub in the butter until the mixture resembles fine breadcrumbs. Add the sugar and sultanas and stir well to combine.

Beat 1 of the eggs, pour it into the flour mixture and bring everything together to a stiff dough. If it's too dry, beat the other egg and add a little at a time.

Tip out the dough on to a lightly floured board or work surface and, using a rolling pin, roll it out until about 5mm thick. (They can be thicker, depending on how you like them!) Using a 5cm round cutter, stamp out 24 rounds of the dough, re-rolling the trimmings as necessary.

Heat a griddle pan over a medium heat until hot, but not smoking. Using a piece of baking paper, carefully butter the griddle to grease. The first Welsh cake will burn slightly while you adjust the heat, so it's worth having a couple of test ones to get the timing and temperature right – a top tip from Jonathan.

Cook the cakes in batches over a medium–low heat, for about 3 minutes on each side, until they are golden brown all over and slightly risen. They need to be closely watched; cook for too long and they easily end up dry.

Transfer the Welsh cakes to a wire cooling rack and leave to cool. Sprinkle with extra caster sugar and, depending on your cholesterol level, put a little pat of Welsh butter on top. Serve with a cup of tea.

Scotti's Honey Biscuits

Our lodger Salvatore keeps his bee hives in our garden, which Scotti, who also lives with us, helps look after. We use their honey in this biscuit recipe, which is akin to a honey digestive. They're wonderful and well worth the trauma of having to look after the bees who seem to want to swarm around our neighbourhood from time to time.

Makes 20

100g salted butter
75g light brown soft sugar
3cm piece of fresh ginger, peeled and grated (about 1 tablespoon)
100g runny honey
250g self-raising flour
1½ tablespoons ground ginger
1 teaspoon bicarbonate of soda
1 egg yolk

Preheat the oven to 190°C/170°C fan/Gas 5. Line two large baking sheets with baking paper.

Place the butter, sugar, ginger and honey in a small pan over a low heat. Allow the butter to melt and the sugar to dissolve, stir, then remove the pan from the heat and leave the mixture to cool.

Sift the flour into a large bowl and add the ground ginger and bicarbonate of soda, stirring to combine. Gradually stir in the cooled honey mixture and the egg yolk. Bring the mixture together and knead it briefly to make a dough.

Using your hands, roll the dough into 20 equal-sized balls, placing the balls on the baking sheets as you go and leaving 3cm between each to allow the biscuits to spread during baking. Bake for 10 minutes, until golden brown. Remove the biscuits from the oven, leave them to cool on the tray for 1 minute, then transfer them to a wire rack to cool completely before serving, or transfer to an airtight container and store for up to 2 days.

Randall's Chocolate Cake

Randall lives across the road from us and is a great baker. At university he worked at a chocolate shop and became the fount of all knowledge on all things chocolate. After being disappointed with so many cakes he came up with this one.

Serves 12

210g plain flour
90g cocoa powder
2 teaspoons bicarbonate
    of soda
1 teaspoon baking powder
1 teaspoon kosher salt
400g caster sugar
250ml soured cream
125ml vegetable oil
2 large eggs
1½ teaspoons vanilla
    extract
125ml freshly brewed hot
    coffee (a strong instant
    coffee is fine)

For the chocolate
    buttercream
125g 54% dark chocolate
    (70% dark chocolate
    is fine, if that's all you
    can find), chopped,
    plus optional extra to
    decorate
200g unsalted butter, at
    room temperature, plus
    extra for greasing
2 teaspoons vanilla extract
1 tablespoon whole milk
125g icing sugar, sifted

Preheat the oven to 180°C/160°C fan/Gas 4. Butter two 20cm (5cm deep) round cake tins and line the base and sides with baking paper.

Sift the flour, cocoa, bicarbonate of soda, baking powder and salt into a bowl. Add the sugar and mix everything together thoroughly with a whisk.

In another bowl, combine the soured cream, oil, eggs and vanilla. Gradually add the wet ingredient mixture to the dry, using a wooden spoon to mix gently after each addition until just combined. Then, add the coffee and stir to combine. Take care not to over-mix – just combining is fine. And don't forget to scrape all the way to the bottom of the bowl. Divide the cake mixture equally between the prepared tins and bake for 40 minutes, until a skewer inserted into the centre of each sponge comes out clean. Cool in the tins for 30 minutes, then turn out the sponges on to a wire rack to cool completely.

Meanwhile, make the buttercream. Place the chocolate in a heatproof bowl set over a pan of gently simmering water. Stir until just melted, then remove from the heat and set the bowl aside until the chocolate has cooled to room temperature.

Beat the butter in the bowl of a stand mixer fitted with the paddle on medium–high speed for about 3 minutes, until light yellow and fluffy. Add the vanilla and milk and beat again for a few minutes. Turn the mixer speed to low and gradually add the icing sugar, then beat at medium speed, scraping down the bowl as necessary, until smooth and creamy. On low speed, add the chocolate to the butter mixture and mix until combined.

Spread about one third of the buttercream in an even layer over the top of one of the sponges and top with the second sponge. Use the remaining buttercream to coat the top and sides of the cake, smoothing it out evenly. Grate a little extra chocolate over the top to decorate, if you wish.

Kate's Preserves

Without a doubt, my neighbour Kate makes the best apricot jam, and we are very fortunate to be on her list of people who receive a jar of each marmalade and jam. I like the old-fashioned way to check if jam is set. Put a saucer in the freezer for 10 minutes, then when you think it's ready, put a bit of your mixture on the saucer. Push a finger through it and if the mixture wrinkles, then it is ready.

Makes 3–4 jars

Seville Orange Marmalade
1.5kg Seville oranges
2kg granulated sugar
juice of 2 large lemons

Scrub the oranges and take off the buttons. Put the oranges in a large preserving pan with 3 litres of cold water. Bring to the boil, then simmer gently for 2½ hours. Carefully remove the oranges, and you should have 1.8 litres of liquid left. If it's less, add cold water to make it up.

When the oranges have cooled, cut them in half. Remove and discard the pips, squeezing any juice into a jug as you go. Pour the juice back into the pan. Cut the orange peel into shreds to suit your preference. I like them quite thick. Put the fruit back into the pan with the cooking liquid. (I often do this at night and then finish things off in the morning.) Add the sugar to the pan and heat the mixture through gently until the sugar has dissolved. Bring the mixture up to a fast boil. Add the lemon juice and boil for 15–20 minutes, until thickened and jam-like. Take the pan off the heat and leave the marmalade for 15 minutes, skimming any scum off the top after that time. Stir gently, then pour it into sterilised, warm jars and seal immediately. The marmalade keeps in a cool, dry place for up to 12 months. Once opened, store it in the fridge and eat it within a month – if you can resist it for that long!

Apricot Jam
1.5kg perfectly ripe, stoned apricots, halved or quartered if they're big
1.1kg granulated sugar
juice of 1–2 lemons, depending on taste

Put the apricots and sugar in a preserving pan. Stir together over a low heat until all the sugar has dissolved. Bring the liquid to a fast boil – it can take a few minutes until you get a proper rolling boil. I start adding lemon juice once the rolling boil is in full swing and then taste as the mixture cooks (you'll know how much you want only if you keep tasting). After the jam has been boiling for about 15 minutes, it should be ready. The fruit will still have its shape, so it's not too jammy, but very fruity.

Take off the heat and leave the jam for 15 minutes, skimming any scum off the top after that time. Pour into sterilised, warm jars. When it's cool, keep it in the fridge. It goes in no time at home, so I've no idea how long it lasts.

Street Party

Sausage Rolls

When you find yourself hosting a street party and catering for about 300-plus people, you need things that are easy to make and simple to prepare in advance, and sausage rolls are perfect for that. Neil is usually in charge of the sausage rolls and he makes brilliant ones.

You want to get good pork and use tons of spices. I like a classic pork sausage roll as it's wonderfully moist, but you could mix it up a bit by using two-thirds game, such as venison, and just one-third pork.

Makes 10

500g pork sausagemeat
a couple of sage leaves, chopped (about 1 teaspoon)
2 or 3 thyme sprigs, leaves picked and chopped (about 1 teaspoon)
½ teaspoon Dijon mustard
1 x 500g block of ready-made puff pastry
flour, for dusting
1 egg, beaten
sea salt and freshly ground black pepper

Put the sausagemeat, sage, thyme and mustard in a large bowl and season with salt and pepper. Using your hands, mix everything together until fully combined. Heat a dry frying pan over a medium heat and fry a small piece of the sausage mixture until cooked. Taste to check for seasoning and adjust the mixture if necessary. Cover and refrigerate until needed.

Cut the puff pastry block in half, then roll out each half on a lightly floured surface to a large rectangle, about 10cm x 30cm.

Remove the sausagemeat from the fridge and divide into two equal pieces. Mould each half into a long sausage shape, positioning each one in the centre of a length of pastry.

With the long edge of the pastry facing you, brush a little beaten egg along the edge of the pastry closest to you. Gently lift the pastry edge farthest from you and fold it over the sausagemeat, bringing the long edges together to meet each other and pressing them to seal. Crimp them together, then trim to neaten.

Line a baking tray with baking paper. Gently lift the sausage rolls into the tray and, using a sharp knife, make slits along the length of each, spacing the slits about 2.5cm apart. Brush them all over with the beaten egg. Chill the sausage rolls in the fridge for about 20 minutes to firm up.

Meanwhile, heat the oven to 200°C/180°C fan/Gas 6.

Bake the sausage rolls for 25 minutes, until the pastry is golden brown and the filling is cooked through. Remove from the oven and allow them to cool for 10 minutes before slicing each long roll into 5 to give 10 sausage rolls.

Scotch Eggs

When we did our very first street party, we put a fryer in our back garden and deep-fried hundreds of Scotch eggs. They were brilliant and everybody loved them and kept coming back for more.

Scotch eggs have had a bit of a renaissance recently, often with slightly eccentric variations on the theme. I think there's a lot to be said for the traditional ways of doing things – a proper egg such as a Burford Brown, proper sausagemeat, deep fried and eaten slightly warm.

Makes 8

10 large free-range eggs
8 pork sausages, meat squeezed out (about 650g sausagemeat)
1 tablespoon chopped sage leaves
1 tablespoon thyme leaves
100g plain flour
150g panko breadcrumbs
2 litres vegetable oil, for deep-frying
sea salt and freshly ground black pepper

Bring a large pan of water to the boil. Add 8 of the eggs and boil them for 5 minutes, then transfer them to a bowl of ice-cold water to stop them cooking. Once cooled, carefully peel them and leave to one side.

Tip the sausagemeat into a bowl. Add the herbs and season. Mix well until fully combined, then divide the mixture into 8 equal-sized balls.

Tip the flour on to a plate. Beat the remaining eggs in a bowl, and tip the breadcrumbs on to a second plate.

Flour your hands, then in the palm of one hand, flatten one of the sausagemeat balls into an oval-shaped patty. Roll a peeled egg in flour, then pop it in the middle of the patty. Gently shape the meat evenly around the egg, moulding it with your hands until you've sealed the egg inside.

Roll the meat-wrapped egg in the flour, shake off any excess, then dip it into the beaten egg, followed by the breadcrumbs to coat. Repeat to coat all the eggs.

Heat the oil in a deep pan (it shouldn't come more than two thirds of the way up the side) or deep-fat fryer to about 160°C. To test if the oil is hot enough, add a pinch of breadcrumbs. If they sizzle and brown after 10 seconds, the oil is ready.

Carefully lower the eggs into the pan and cook them for 6 minutes, or until golden brown, turning them every so often so that they colour evenly. Remove the eggs with a slotted spoon and set them aside to drain on kitchen paper.

To serve, slice open each scotch egg and season with a touch of salt and pepper.

Asparagus Quiche

Some people think that you are allowed to put anything you want on a quiche. But I'm not so sure. It is actually quite hard to make a good quiche and one of the best quiches that I've ever eaten was made from a Simon Hopkinson recipe – it was just onions, onions and more onions and cream and cheese.

This is an asparagus quiche, but you could use broccoli if asparagus isn't in season. You could vary the cheese you use, but you do need a hard, firm cheese. So perhaps Comté or Gruyère, or even a hard blue. You could also add a bit of cumin. Use this egg to cream ratio and you have yourself the perfect quiche base upon which to carefully build other flavours without going crazy.

Serves 6–8

For the pastry
170g plain flour, plus extra
    for dusting
pinch of salt
50g lard
50g unsalted butter
1 egg yolk
2 tablespoons iced water

For the filling
2 bunches of asparagus
    (about 800g) or 200g
    purple sprouting
    broccoli
15g salted butter
1 banana shallot
1 garlic clove
3 egg yolks
1 egg
200ml double cream
200g cheddar cheese,
    grated
sea salt and freshly
    ground black pepper

crisp green salad, to serve
    (optional)

First, make the pastry. Sift the flour into a large bowl and add the pinch of salt. Add the lard and butter and rub them in with your fingertips, until the mixture resembles breadcrumbs.

Mix the egg yolk with the water and lightly whisk, then add to the flour mix and use the back of a knife to combine, then use your hands to bring the mixture together to a firm dough.

Tip out the dough onto a lightly floured board or work surface and knead it gently. Cover or wrap it in cling film and transfer it to the fridge to rest for at least 20 minutes.

While the pastry rests, prepare the vegetables for the filling. If you're using asparagus, snap off the woody stems (feel along the stem until it bends) and blanch them in boiling salted water for about 2 minutes (depending upon the thickness of the asparagus), until just cooked. Drain well. If you're using broccoli, trim the stems and blanch them in salted boiling water for 2 minutes, until just cooked, then drain well.

Heat the oven to 200°C/180°C fan/Gas 6.

Roll out the rested dough on a lightly floured board or work surface to a 25cm disc about the thickness of a £1 coin (about 3mm). Carefully use the pastry disc to line a 20cm, loose-bottomed fluted tart tin, pushing the pastry into the edges and grooves. Trim the excess to neaten. Chill the tart case in the fridge for 20 minutes.

Prick the base of the chilled tart case all over with a fork, then line it with scrunched-up baking paper and pour in some baking beans (or use dried beans or uncooked rice, if you don't have baking beans – you can reuse the beans, but don't eat them!). Blind bake the pastry case for 20 minutes, until lightly golden, then remove the paper and beans and return the case to the oven for a further 5 minutes, until golden brown. Remove from the oven and allow to cool slightly in the tin.

Turn the oven down to 180°C/160°C fan/Gas 4.

While the tart case is cooling a little, make the filling. In a pan, add the butter and cook the shallot and garlic for about 10 minutes, until soft but not coloured. Transfer to a bowl and leave to cool, then add the egg yolks, egg, cream and cheese to the bowl. Give it all a good mix to break up the eggs and combine the ingredients, and season with salt and pepper.

Line the base of the pastry case with broccoli or asparagus, then pour in the egg and cheese mixture. Bake the quiche for 25 minutes, until the filling is set to the touch and golden brown. Allow to cool slightly, then remove it from the tin to serve. I like to serve it slightly warm, with a crisp green salad on the side.

Barbecued Curried Monkfish Tails

Curried monkfish is always a winner. Marinate the fish in loads of yoghurt, loads of spices and it will be ready for barbecuing and perfect for feeding a hungry crowd. I place it straight on the grill and serve it with a lovely curry sauce, but it could also be served along with a refreshing salad – it's up to you.

When we did this for one of our street parties we had about 20 barbecues, and three different kitchens on the go. This monkfish was the out and out favourite dish!

No other firm-fleshed fish is quite as good as monkfish for this recipe, so monkfish it will have to be. But you could experiment with how you treat your monkfish – perhaps cut it into rounds or skewer it for kebabs.

Serves 6+

1 teaspoon ground turmeric
juice and finely grated zest of 2 unwaxed limes
200g full-fat plain yoghurt
a large pinch of sea salt
2 monkfish tails, about 600g each, cut into 200g portions
2 spring onions, sliced

For the sauce
1 tablespoon olive oil
2 garlic cloves, finely chopped
5cm piece of fresh ginger, grated
½ teaspoon cumin seeds, crushed
½ teaspoon fenugreek seeds, crushed
½ teaspoon ground turmeric
1 green chilli, deseeded and finely chopped
1 tablespoon smoked harissa paste
4 ripe plum tomatoes, or use tinned
a handful of coriander, leaves and tender stems picked and chopped

Combine the turmeric, lime juice and zest, yoghurt and salt in a large bowl. Add the fish and turn to coat, then refrigerate for at least 1 hour.

Meanwhile, heat your barbecue grill to hot.

Towards the end of the chilling time, make the sauce. Heat the oil in a medium pan over a low heat. When hot, add the garlic and ginger and cook for 1 minute. Add the cumin, fenugreek, turmeric, chilli and harissa paste, and toast in the pan, stirring, for 1–2 minutes to release the flavours. Add the tomatoes and cook for 10 minutes, until they start to break down and form a sauce. Finish with the chopped coriander.

Grill the monkfish tails on the hot barbecue for about 5 minutes, turning, until a knife goes through the thickest parts easily and the fish is cooked through. Allow the fish to rest for 2 minutes, then serve with the curried sauce poured over and sprinkled with the spring-onion slices.

Barbecued Rib-eye Steak with Tomato Salad

This is a dish I've used at all our street parties. It's an easy barbecue recipe and an all-time favourite. You just need rocket, watercress and a very good steak.

If there's ever a choice, then rib-eye is my favourite cut of steak, partly because of the ratio of fat to meat. I love it so much I had it at my wedding. I'm not a chef who wants my steak rare or bloody – medium or medium rare is perfect for me and rib-eye can be cooked like that without it turning out tough, and I think it's just delicious. I love the flavour that the bone gives to the meat. You could also use sirloin or rump, or a t-bone steak if you want a thinner slice.

Serves 12

4 rib steaks (about
    800–900g each), bone
    in, if possible, at room
    temperature
vegetable oil, for rubbing
a handful of watercress and
    rocket salad, to serve
sea salt and freshly ground
    black pepper

For the tomato salad
2 teaspoons Dijon mustard
100ml extra-virgin olive oil
25ml red wine vinegar
1 garlic clove, peeled
4 ox-heart or beef
    tomatoes, sliced
1 red onion, thinly sliced
a handful of basil, leaves
    picked

Prepare your barbecue so that it's at the right temperature to cook, but not burn the meat. When the coals are white, they are hot enough to use.

Gently rub the steaks with a touch of vegetable oil, then season with salt and pepper and chargrill for at least 15 minutes, turning them over and moving them around the grill as needed, until evenly coloured but not burnt.

Move the steaks to one side, away from the fiercest heat, so that they do not scorch. Using a skewer or very thin-bladed knife, pierce the steaks and touch the blade to your lips – if it's hot the steaks are done. Transfer them to a plate, and leave them to rest for 15 minutes, covered loosely with foil.

Meanwhile, make the tomato salad. Mix the mustard with the olive oil and vinegar. Then, using a microplane, slice the garlic very finely. Add it to the mustard, oil and vinegar and stir to combine to a dressing.

Mix the tomatoes with the red onion in a bowl, season with salt and pepper, then pour the dressing over the top. Set aside to marinate, until you're ready to serve.

Once the steaks have rested, it's time to carve them. Remove the meat from the bone (if necessary), and slice against the grain to give about 2cm-thick slices. Divide the tomato salad equally between serving plates and scatter over the basil leaves. Place the sliced steak on top of the tomatoes and garnish with some watercress and rocket. Alternatively, serve the sliced steak and the salad on a large serving platter and allow everyone to help themselves.

We've had about three street parties where we live in Spitalfields. They've been huge fun and great successes. All the food comes out of our kitchen with the help of the Spitalfields Society and our neighbours who contribute massively to the festivities. I would guess about 350 people or so come out on to the street to mingle, eat and drink. We have some great neighbourhood restaurants who set up little food stands – Hawksmoor, St. John's, Wright Brothers who shuck hundreds of oysters, and TRADE who do lovely pastrami. I tend to make loads of salads and great big trifles – basically anything that's easy to prepare and convenient to serve on a platter for people to eat *en masse*. And everyone eats like gannets – you'd think they hadn't seen food before. But it's so much fun and a great community thing.

Anyone can organise a street party, and it's great to get everyone to contribute. There's a cake competition and a pet competition – it's actually more like a village fete than anything else, except that it's set on inner city London streets. In fact, I once had to judge the cake competition and nearly upset half the neighbourhood.

Lemon Butterfly Cakes

A butterfly cake is similar to a fairy cake. You just slice the top off the cake, cut that in half, then generously buttercream the top of the uncut cake and place the top halves back on like wings. A butterfly. These were probably the first things I ever made as a kid and while most people have gone fancy with cupcakes, I like to keep things classic. The lemon in the buttercream brings lightness.

Makes 24

200g unsalted butter, softened
200g caster sugar
4 large eggs, beaten
200g self-raising flour
finely grated zest of
    1 unwaxed lemon
a pinch of salt
2 tablespoons whole milk

For the buttercream
250g icing sugar, sifted, plus extra for dusting
125g unsalted butter, softened
finely grated zest of
    1 unwaxed lemon
    and juice of ¼

Preheat the oven to 180°C/160°C fan/Gas 4 and line a two 12-hole muffin tins with 24 paper cases (if you have only one tin, cook the cakes in two batches).

In a large bowl, cream together the butter and sugar, until the mixture is pale and fluffy. Add the beaten eggs, a little at a time, beating well after each addition. If the mixture starts to split, add a tablespoon of flour and beat again. Add the lemon zest.

Sift the flour and salt over the mixture and fold in with a spatula, until no streaks remain. Finally, fold in the milk.

Using two dessertspoons (one to scoop and the other to push the mixture into each paper case), half fill the paper cases, making sure you have an equal amount of batter in each.

Bake the fairy cakes for 15 minutes, until they are golden brown and spring back when you gently press down on them. Allow them to cool in the tin until cool enough to handle, then transfer them to a wire rack to cool completely.

While the cakes are cooling, make the buttercream. Beat together the icing sugar and butter in a bowl, then add the lemon zest and juice and beat again until light, fluffy and fully combined.

Once the fairy cakes are cooled, using a sharp serrated knife, cut off the top of each one and pipe or spoon in a generous amount of buttercream. Cut the tops in half and position the two halves on top of the buttercream filling to look like wings. Dust with icing sugar to finish.

Victoria Sponge

The secret to a good Victoria sponge is a hot oven and ensuring that you use the right tin – not too small and not too large. Two 20cm tins are perfect.

I like to fill the middle with fresh fruit rather than jam, so for me summer is the best time for a Victoria sponge cake. I use strawberries but raspberries are great, or even mulberries if you can get them.

Serves 10

For the sponges
200g self-raising flour
1 teaspoon baking powder
200g caster sugar
200g unsalted butter, softened, plus extra for greasing
4 large eggs

For the filling
200g strawberries, hulled and quartered
50g caster sugar
200ml double cream
¼ vanilla pod, seeds scraped out, or 1 teaspoon vanilla essence

icing sugar, to dust

Preheat the oven to 180°C/160°C fan/Gas 4. Use a little bit of baking paper to rub a little butter around the inside of two 20cm cake tins, until the sides and base are lightly coated, then line the base with a circle of baking paper.

Make the sponges. Sift the flour and baking powder together into a bowl and leave to one side.

In a large bowl, add the sugar and butter and, using a hand-held electric whisk, cream them together until light and fluffy.

Crack the eggs into a separate bowl and beat them together using a fork. Add the beaten eggs to the sugar and butter a little at a time, whisking well after each addition.

Using a spatula, gently fold the flour mixture into the egg mixture, being careful not to over-mix.

Divide the batter equally between the tins, scraping all of it from the bowl with a spatula and using the spatula to gently smooth the surface. Use a dessert spoon to make a slight hollow in the centre of each portion of batter – this will make sure you have level sponges.

Bake the sponges on the middle shelf of the oven for 25 minutes, until golden brown, springy to the touch, and coming away from the edge of the tins.

While the sponges are baking, prepare the strawberries. Tip the strawberry pieces into a large bowl and stir through half the caster sugar. Leave to one side.

Using a hand-held electric whisk, whip the cream with the remaining sugar and the vanilla until it holds soft peaks.

When the sponges are ready, set them aside to cool in their tins for 5 minutes, then run a palette knife around the inside edge of the tins and carefully turn out the sponges onto a wire cooling rack. Leave to cool completely.

To assemble the cake, place one sponge upside down on a serving plate and spread it with plenty of the vanilla cream. Don't spread it right to the edges – leave a small gap. Add the chopped strawberries on top along with any of the juices, then top with the second cake, bottom downwards. Sprinkle over the icing sugar and you're ready to serve.

Fruit Scones

I always make scones for our street parties, just because I love them and also because we always have loads of leftover jams in the cupboard. And that's because I'm fortunate enough to have been given many gifts of various Fortnum's jams over the years. A scone is a great way to use them up.

This recipe is an adaptation of Delia's. With something so classic you need only go to the best and Delia Smith is one of the very best. I've tweaked her recipe a bit with the addition of baking powder to give the scones elevation and make them slightly lighter.

Makes 12

500g self-raising flour
2 teaspoons baking powder
100g unsalted butter, cubed
and chilled
50g caster sugar
50g sultanas
2 eggs
240ml whole milk, plus
extra for brushing
strawberry jam and clotted
cream, to serve

Preheat the oven to 220°C/200°C fan/Gas 7. Line two baking sheets with baking paper.

Sift the flour and baking powder into a large bowl. Add the butter and, using your fingertips, rub it in until the mixture resembles breadcrumbs. Add the sugar and sultanas and mix well.

Crack the eggs into a measuring jug, add the milk and whisk everything together with a fork. Little by little, add the wet ingredients into the dry ingredients, using a table knife to combine the mixture to a soft, sticky dough.

Turn out the dough on to a lightly floured work surface, knead it lightly and pat it into a round, about 3cm thick.

Using a 5cm round cutter, cut out as many scones as possible from the dough, re-combining and flattening the trimmings as necessary.

Evenly space the scones on the prepared baking sheets. Brush the tops with a little extra milk and bake them for 12–15 minutes, or until they are well risen and a pale, golden-brown colour. Remove from the oven and transfer to a wire rack to cool. Serve with jam and clotted cream.

Sweets

Queen of Puddings

I love a queen of puddings. Breadcrumbs, soaked in milk, vanilla flavoured egg, jam on top and then meringue. And when made well, it's delicious. It's also a great way to use up old bread or leftover jams, so it's basically a store cupboard essential. Don't use a sugary jam as the whole thing will then become overpoweringly sweet.

Serves 6

25g unsalted butter, plus extra for greasing
570ml whole milk
100g fresh white breadcrumbs
3 eggs, separated
100g caster sugar
finely grated zest of 1 unwaxed lemon
5 tablespoons raspberry jam
single cream, to serve

Preheat the oven to 170°C/150°C fan/Gas 3 and grease a 24cm oval oven-proof serving dish with a little butter.

Heat the milk a saucepan over a low heat until gently warmed. Put the breadcrumbs into a bowl, pour over the milk and leave the breadcrumbs to soak for 30 minutes until all the liquid has been absorbed.

Beat the egg yolks lightly with a fork, then add them to the soaked breadcrumbs along with 50g of the caster sugar, the 25g of butter and the lemon zest. Stir to combine thoroughly then transfer to the serving dish and bake for 20–25 minutes, until golden brown and set. Remove from the oven and leave to cool.

Reduce the oven temperature to 140°C/120°C fan/Gas 1.

Gently warm the jam in a small pan to loosen it and spread evenly over the set breadcrumbs.

Tip the egg whites into a clean bowl and, using a hand-held electric whisk, whisk to soft peaks. Add the remaining 175g of caster sugar a little at a time, whisking between each addition, until you have a lovely, glossy meringue that holds soft peaks. Spoon the meringue over the top of the jam, using the spoon to make little peaks – like the peaks of the queen's crown – or you can put the meringue into a piping bag and pipe it over the top.

Bake the pudding for a further 30 minutes, until the meringue is golden brown. Serve with cream while still warm.

Apple Tart

The inspiration for this fantastic tart came from the celebrated American chef Alice Waters who owns Chez Panisse in Berkeley, California. I first ate there about 20 years ago, and have huge respect for Alice and everything she's done at her restaurant.

This is a French classic using a really short pastry topped with apples, quite similar to an apple galette. You could use apples, peaches or figs for this recipe – they all work really well. It's important not to use fruit that's too soft or too ripe as the pastry base takes a while to cook and you'd find yourself ending up with a fruit mush.

Serves 8

280g plain flour
a pinch of salt
170g unsalted butter, cut into cubes and chilled, plus an extra 50g (melted) for brushing
about 100ml ice-cold water
8 apples
100g caster sugar, plus extra for sprinkling
vanilla ice cream or double cream, to serve

Preheat the oven to 190°C/170°C fan/Gas 5.

In a large bowl, sift together the flour and salt. Add the cubed butter and use your fingertips to rub it into the flour until it resembles fine breadcrumbs, with flecks of whole butter still visible (the pastry will be very short). Little by little, add the water, just enough until the pastry comes together into a ball – take care not to overwork it. Form the pastry into a ball and flatten it slightly, then wrap it in cling film and place it in the fridge to rest for 1 hour.

Dust a large sheet of baking paper with flour. Remove the pastry from the fridge and roll it out to a 25cm circle. Gently transfer the pastry circle to the baking tray and prick the base with a fork. Leave the pastry case to rest in the fridge while you prepare the apples.

Peel, core and quarter the apples, then slice each quarter into about 6 pieces.

Line the pastry case with apple slices, beginning around the outside edge and fanning the apples, slightly overlapping, in decreasing concentric circles towards the centre, until you have covered the bottom of the case. Brush the apples with the melted butter, then sprinkle over the sugar.

Bake the tart for about 40 minutes, until the pastry edges and apple filling are golden brown. Sprinkle a little more sugar over the top and serve with vanilla ice cream or double cream.

Paris Brest

I've included this dessert in the book because Neil is a massive cyclist and the history of this recipe is all about the Paris-Brest-Paris cycle race. The shape of the dish is a representation of a bike wheel, whilst the almonds on top represent cobbled French streets.

It looks much harder to make than it actually is and it's a great one to serve at home for friends, either as individual desserts or as one great big bike wheel.

Makes 8

For the praline paste and caramelised hazelnuts
150g whole blanched hazelnuts
125g caster sugar
5ml hazelnut oil

For the choux pastry
½ small pinch of salt
a good pinch of caster sugar
50g unsalted butter
70g plain flour, sifted
3 large eggs
50g flaked almonds

For the chocolate sauce
small pinch of sea salt
30g caster sugar
125g 70% dark chocolate, broken into pieces

To finish
250ml double cream
icing sugar

First, prepare the praline paste and caramelised hazelnuts. Heat the oven to 200°C/180°C fan/Gas 6 and line a baking sheet with baking paper.

Scatter the nuts into a separate baking tray and place them in the oven to roast for 8–10 minutes, until lightly golden. Transfer the nuts to a heavy-based pan. Place over a low heat and gradually add the sugar. Cook, stirring continuously, to a golden caramel. Remove from the heat.

Pour the caramelised nuts over the lined baking sheet and, using a fork (don't use your fingers – the caramel will be scalding hot), separate out 32 individual nuts. Leave them to cool and harden, then transfer them to an airtight container until needed.

Once the remaining sheet of caramelised nuts has cooled (about 30 minutes or so), break it up into pieces, transfer it to a food processor add the hazelnut oil and blitz it to a smooth praline paste. Transfer the paste to an airtight container and leave it at room temperature until needed.

Next, prepare the choux pastry. Heat the oven to 200°C/180°C fan/Gas 6. Line a baking sheet with baking paper and use an 8cm-diameter glass or pastry cutter to draw 8 circles, evenly spaced, over the paper. Turn over the paper so that the pencil markings are on the underside.

Pour 150ml of water into a medium saucepan and add the salt, sugar and butter. Place the pan over a medium heat and allow the butter to melt and the mixture to heat up. Stir to combine, then tip in the flour in one go and whisk immediately to combine. Increase the heat to high and beat the mixture vigorously with a wooden spoon for about 3–5 minutes, until it comes away from the side of the pan.

Transfer the dough to a stand mixer fitted with the paddle attachment and beat on medium speed for about 5–8 minutes, until the dough is cool enough that it won't cook the eggs. One at a time, add two of the eggs and beat until the mixture just holds it shape on the paddle and is lovely and smooth and shiny. Transfer the mixture to a piping bag fitted with a 2cm plain nozzle.

Using the circles on the prepared baking paper as a guide, pipe 8 choux-pastry rings.

Beat the remaining egg and gently egg wash each ring and top each with a sprinkling of the flaked almonds. Bake in the oven for 15 minutes, then turn the tray around and bake for a further 15 minutes, until the rings are evenly baked and golden brown.

Remove the choux rings from the oven and, using a fine skewer or a cocktail stick, puncture a small hole in each ring to allow the steam to escape (this stops the rings going soggy), transferring them to a wire rack to cool completely as you go. Once cool, place them in an airtight container to store until you're ready to serve.

Just before you're ready to serve, make the chocolate sauce. Pour 175ml of water into a small pan and add the salt and sugar. Place the pan over a medium heat and bring the liquid to a simmer. Turn the heat down as low as possible and whisk in the chocolate. Cook for 4–5 minutes, until the sauce is the consistency of double cream and coats the back of a spoon. Pour the sauce into a jug and keep warm.

Meanwhile, lightly whip the double cream with 1 teaspoon of the praline paste to soft peaks and spoon it into a piping bag fitted with a 1cm star nozzle.

Halve each choux ring horizontally and pipe equal amounts of the cream on top of the bottom half of each. Top with 4 caramelised hazelnuts per ring, then drizzle with a tablespoon of the praline paste. Top with the ring lids and dust with icing sugar. Serve with the warm chocolate sauce alongside for your guests to pour over as they wish.

Summer Pudding

We all love summer pudding though it seems harder to make well these days as it's tricky to get the blackcurrants, redcurrants and white currants that you need. But it's well worth the effort trying to hunt them down.

   You must use white bread but it doesn't need to be fancy bread. The key is to ensure the bread is almost invisible from being soaked in the fruits' juices. Nor should the pudding be overly sweet but should have a tart edge, which is why a carefully curated mix of different fruits, black and white currants in particular, is so important. If you can get all this right then you will have made one of the greatest desserts known to humankind.

Serves 8

100g strawberries, hulled
    and quartered
200g redcurrants
200g blackcurrants
400g raspberries
150g caster sugar
unsalted butter, for
    greasing
8 slices of white bread,
    crusts removed
icing sugar, for dusting
250g thick double cream,
    to serve

Put all the berries in a large saucepan with the sugar and gently heat for about 3 minutes to dissolve the sugar – take care not to overheat the pan. You don't want the fruit to cook. Remove the pan from the heat.

Lightly grease a 1-litre pudding basin with unsalted butter.

Trim 1 slice of bread so that it fits at the bottom of the basin. Line the inside of the basin with all but one of the remaining slices, trimming each slice to fit in a single layer with no gaps (fill any gaps with trimmings if necessary).

Reserve 2 tablespoons of the fruit syrup and set it aside in the fridge until you're ready to serve. Pour the fruit and remaining syrup into the bread-lined basin. Use the final slice of bread to seal the top of the pudding.

Cover the pudding with baking paper and top with a saucer or plate that fits exactly into the basin opening. Then, add a 2kg weight on top and leave the pudding in the fridge overnight.

When you're ready to serve, use a knife to loosen the pudding around the edges and turn it out on to a serving plate. Spoon the reserved juices on to the pudding to ensure all the bread is covered and soaked in the juices. Dust with icing sugar and serve with the double cream.

Gâteau Basque

Neil made this fantastic 'cake' the night we had multi-Michelin-starred chefs Phil Howard and Bruce Poole over for supper. It was the perfect dessert to follow the turbot (see page 116). It was a night to go all-out and impress. We needed to do it properly, so game faces were on! We had a pasta dish to start, the turbot for main and then the majestic Gâteau Basque for dessert. It's a beautiful thing, not too sweet and I love it.

This recipe needs a bit of planning, as you'll need to marinate the prunes for a month before you're ready to cook. The results are worth it, though! Any leftovers are great with coffee the next day.

Serves 8–10

For the marinated prunes
90g caster sugar
1 teaspoon Earl Grey tea leaves or 1 Earl Grey tea bag
180g prunes, pitted
125g Armagnac

For the pastry
250g plain flour, sifted
1 teaspoon baking powder
100g ground almonds
a pinch of salt
200g unsalted butter, softened
½ vanilla pod, seeds scraped, pod reserved
180g caster sugar
4 eggs, 3 whole, 1 beaten

For the Basque filling
250ml whole milk
50ml double cream
finely grated zest of ½ lemon
½ vanilla pod, split open, seeds scraped out
60g egg yolks (3–4 egg yolks, depending on the size)

First, marinate the prunes. Measure 425ml of water into a pan and add the sugar. Place the pan over a high heat and bring the water to the boil. Add the tea leaves or the contents of the tea bag and leave to infuse for 2 minutes. Place the prunes in an airtight container, then strain the infusion over the top (discard the tea leaves in the strainer). Cover and allow to cool. Once cool, add the Armagnac and marinate for 1 month.

When you're ready to bake, make the pastry. Place the plain flour, baking powder, ground almonds and salt into a bowl and combine. Set aside.

Tip the butter and vanilla seeds into the bowl of a stand mixer fitted with the beater attachment and beat until smooth. Add the caster sugar and beat again to a smooth paste. One at a time, add 3 of the eggs, beating slowly and making sure that the mixture does not split and is fully combined (if the mixture does split, don't worry – just add a tablespoon of the flour mixture and mix again).

Remove the bowl from the machine and fold in the flour mixture until you have a smooth ball of dough. Form the dough into a block, wrap it in cling film and refrigerate for 2–3 hours to rest.

Meanwhile, make the Basque filling. Place the milk, cream, lemon zest and the scraped vanilla pod and seeds into a medium saucepan over a medium heat. Bring the mixture to just under a boil.

75g caster sugar
15g plain flour
20g semolina
20ml dark rum

You will need a 20cm tart
tin that's 3cm deep.

While the milk mixture is heating up, in a separate bowl, whisk together the egg yolks and caster sugar until pale, then mix in the flour and semolina until smooth.

Add one third of the hot milk mixture to the egg-yolk mixture and stir to combine, then pass it through a sieve back into the pan with the remaining milk mixture to form a custard. Bring the custard back to the boil, stirring continuously, then reduce the heat to a simmer and cook for 5–7 minutes, until thickened.

Remove the custard from the heat and pour it into a shallow tray to cool rapidly. Once it is cold, spoon it into a mixing bowl and add the rum. Beat with a wooden spoon until smooth, then cover with parchment or cling film and refrigerate the filling until needed.

Preheat the oven to 180°C/160°C fan/Gas 4.

Divide the rested dough into 2 pieces of one third and two thirds. Return the smaller piece to the fridge to keep chilled. Roll out the larger piece on a floured work surface to a circle roughly 28cm in diameter and about 3mm thick. Use this piece to line the tart tin, pressing the pastry neatly into all the edges, then chill the pastry case in the fridge for 15 minutes. It will feel thick and cake-like, unlike a traditional pastry.

Once chilled, spoon the Basque filling into a piping bag, without a nozzle attachment, and pipe the mixture into the bottom of the tart case (alternatively, just spoon it in). Drain the marinated prunes and place the prunes into the Basque filling. Roll out the smaller piece of pastry to a circle about 23cm in diameter and 3mm thick. Carefully lift the pastry circle over the tart to form a lid, sealing it at the edges. Trim to neaten, then use the beaten egg to brush over the top as a wash. Score a few holes in the pie lid and bake for 40–45 minutes, until golden brown. Serve at room temperature.

Poached Apricots with Ricotta

We used to serve this at Lime Wood where it was always very popular. We'd whip up a load of ricotta with mascarpone, icing sugar and vanilla and cover it with delicious poached fruits and then top with nuts. It's very Italian and wonderfully simple with loads of fruit and shouldn't be overly sweet – which is why I like it.

You could use any poached stone fruits, such as pears or peaches, but my preference is for apricots.

Serves 6

175g caster sugar
1 clove
1 star anise
½ vanilla pod, split lengthways, seeds scraped out and pod and seeds reserved
12 apricots, halved and stoned
300g ricotta cheese
100g mascarpone
100g icing sugar
a small handful of pistachios, roughly chopped

Pour 400ml of water into a large pan and place it over a medium heat. Add the sugar and whole spices, including the scraped vanilla pod (reserve the seeds). Bring the liquid to the boil, then reduce the heat to low and simmer to dissolve the sugar. Add the apricots and leave them to poach for 10 minutes, until soft. Turn off the heat and allow the fruit to cool in the syrup.

Tip the ricotta into a bowl and beat it together with the mascarpone, icing sugar and vanilla seeds.

To serve, place spoonfuls of the ricotta mixture on to each serving plate and top with equal amounts of the apricots. Spoon over some of the syrup and finish with the chopped pistachios.

Pump Street Chocolate Mousse

This is one of Neil's recipes. Pump Street is a father- and daughter-owned bakery and chocolate-maker in Orford, Suffolk. They use cocoa beans imported from cooperatives around the world to make their craft chocolate. It's fancy chocolate. I once said to Chris, the owner, that he should add a generic milk chocolate bar to his range – and he has! So I'd recommend getting some to make this chocolate mousse extra special. It's a classic mousse and everyone we make this for loves it.

Makes 10–12 individual pots

300g 70% dark chocolate, broken into small pieces
570ml whipping cream
75ml dark rum
200g caster sugar
5 egg whites
a pinch of sea salt

Place the chocolate in a heatproof bowl set over a pan of simmering water, stirring from time to time, until melted. Remove from the heat and set aside.

In a separate bowl, lightly whip the cream to soft peaks and add the rum, gently whisking to combine. Set aside.

Place the sugar in a small saucepan and add just enough water – roughly around 4 tablespoons – to cover. Place the pan over a low–medium heat and allow the sugar to dissolve, swirling the pan from time to time, but don't stir. Bring the syrup to the boil and allow it to reach 120°C on a sugar thermometer.

Meanwhile, place the egg whites in the very clean and dry bowl of a stand mixer fitted with the whisk, and add the salt. When the temperature of the syrup reaches 110°C, start whisking the eggs on medium speed. Then, when the syrup is ready, slowly pour it into the whites, whisking all the time until the meringue holds stiff peaks.

Remove the bowl from the mixer and add the melted chocolate, using a balloon whisk to combine. Then, whisk in the flavoured cream.

Pour the mousse equally into your small serving glasses or pots and refrigerate for 2 hours to set before serving.

Floating Islands

My Uncle Ren has always loved this dessert, so when I was making it for the photography shoot for this book, I called him up and asked him over. It was during lockdown (when we could meet outside), so he didn't come near us, but just enjoyed it quietly in the garden, packed the rest into a container and left for his home, very happy and full!

I like to serve this when I want a bit of a showstopper; the meringue quenelles, the caramel and the custard make it a great dessert to impress.

Serves 8

For the crème anglaise
750ml whole milk
1 vanilla pod, split
    lengthways and seeds
    scraped out
8 egg yolks
200g caster sugar

For the poaching liquor
500ml whole milk
1 tablespoon caster sugar

For the meringue
8 egg whites
200g caster sugar

For the caramel
100g caster sugar

First, make the crème anglaise. Pour the milk into a saucepan and add the vanilla pod. Place it over a medium heat and leave it to heat up, so that the milk infuses with vanilla, until the milk is just below boiling point (look for a few bubbles around the edges).

Meanwhile, whisk together the egg yolks and sugar in a mixing bowl until pale. Pour a touch of the hot milk mixture on to the eggs and sugar, and whisk rapidly until smooth. Pour the egg mixture into the pan with the rest of the milk. Stir continuously over a medium heat for 4–5 minutes, or until the mixture has thickened enough to coat the back of a spoon.

Strain the mixture through a sieve into a bowl, cover the surface with a piece of baking paper to stop a skin forming and leave the crème anglaise to cool (this is quickest set into a bowl of ice). Once cool, transfer the crème anglaise to the fridge until needed.

Make the poaching liquor. Combine the milk, sugar and 250ml of water in a wide pan that's deep enough to accommodate 3–4 meringue quenelles at a time. Place it over a low heat, stirring to dissolve the sugar.

Meanwhile, make the meringue. Tip the egg whites into a large bowl and, using an electric hand whisk, whisk them until they form stiff peaks (but don't let them go dry). Add 1 tablespoon of the sugar, and continue to whisk until the mixture comes back to stiff peaks. Keep adding the sugar, a tablespoon at a time, whisking between each addition until you've added all of it and you have a thick, glossy meringue.

Using a serving spoon dipped in cold water, shape 12–16 (depending on the size of your spoon) quenelles (oval shapes with pointed ends) of the meringue and gently poach them in the milk mixture about 3–4 at a time. You need to leave room to be able to flip them over. Cook the quenelles for 4 minutes each side, making sure the liquid doesn't boil, otherwise the meringues will puff and then collapse. As each meringue is cooked, remove it from the poaching liquid with a slotted spoon and place it on a large tray lined with baking paper to cool.

Make the caramel. Tip the sugar into a clean pan and add 2 teaspoons of water. Melt the sugar over a low heat, brushing down the sides of the pan with a pastry brush from time to time, until the sugar turns a dark copper colour. Do not stir! Remove the caramel immediately from the heat to stop it from burning.

Pour the caramel over the meringues and leave until set.

To serve, make a generous pool of crème anglaise on each serving plate and top it with a meringue.

Strawberry Ice Cream

We were visiting chef and restaurateur Mitch Tonks in Devon and went to stay with some friends, Martha and Peter, just outside Dartmouth. One night we were playing cards and Martha brought out the most delicious strawberry ice cream. I said that I had to have the recipe. Martha used to work with the legendary chef Joyce Molyneux at The Carved Angel in Dartmouth and the recipe is inspired by Joyce's belief in simplicity and traditional methods. It's a great way to use up a glut of strawberries and is so delicious.

Serves 8–10

500g ripe, sweet strawberries, hulled and quartered
100g caster sugar
300ml double cream
juice of 1 lemon, plus extra if needed

Put the strawberries and half the sugar into a bowl, cover and leave the strawberries to macerate for 4 hours.

Put the macerated strawberries, along with the cream, lemon juice and remaining sugar into a blender and blitz until smooth. Taste and add a touch more lemon juice, if needed.

Churn the mixture in an ice-cream machine according to the manufacturer's instructions, until set, then transfer it to a freezerproof container and freeze until needed.

If you don't have an ice-cream machine, transfer the ice-cream mixture to a freezerproof container and freeze it for 2 hours, until just starting to set around the edges. Remove it from the freezer and churn it either by beating it with an electric whisk or whisking by hand. Place the ice cream back in the freezer, then repeat the process three more times (the whole process will take about 4 hours and you will need to do this every hour to remove any crystals), after which it should be perfectly smooth and you can just pop it back in the freezer and leave it until you're ready to use.

Take the ice cream out of the freezer to soften up for about 10 minutes before you want to serve it.

Shortbread

There is no shortbread like Borthwick's! Neil just makes the best shortbread. The key, he says, is lots of butter and then cooking it at just the right temperature. I like a tiny bit of colour on mine, but not much or it will become too firm and won't melt in your mouth.

Shortbread always reminds me of a great time we had in Scotland with our friends, the chefs Fergus and Margot Henderson, where we passed an afternoon dunking shortbread into glasses of Laphroaig single malt whisky – it was like enjoying an after-dinner drink with petit fours but rather more full-on!

Makes 16 fingers

250g unsalted butter, cubed and chilled
325g plain flour
100g caster sugar, plus extra for sprinkling

Preheat the oven to 160°C/140°C fan/Gas 2–3. Line a 30cm x 20cm baking tray with baking paper.

Place all the ingredients in a mixing bowl and use your fingertips to rub them together, until the mixture resembles breadcrumbs. Bring the mixture together into a dough, then transfer it to the prepared baking tray and press it out into an even layer, reaching it all the way into the corners. Prick the dough all over with a fork.

Bake the biscuit sheet for 40 minutes, until golden and cooked through, then allow it to cool for 10 minutes. Sprinkle liberally with caster sugar and cut the biscuit into fingers while it's still warm. Leave the shortbreads to cool completely, then transfer them to an airtight container and store for up to 1 week.

Soda Bread

A few years past we went to stay with our friends Pat Llewellyn and Ben Adler at their cottage in Carmarthenshire. Whilst staying there I made large batches of soda bread as there was no local bakery. There was also no internet connection, so we would spend much of our time at the local village pub enjoying a drink or two, playing cards and checking emails. Whilst there, and a few drinks in, Neil would regularly barter away my bread for freshly caught fish or other produce from the locals. So, our meals at the cottage turned into wonderful celebrations of the best of west Wales produce. We were truly eating local.

Makes 1 loaf

150g wholemeal flour
300g strong plain white flour, plus extra for kneading
1 teaspoon bicarbonate of soda
½ teaspoon salt
300ml buttermilk
1 teaspoon black treacle
1 teaspoon honey

Heat the oven to 200°C/180°C fan/Gas 6 and line a baking tray with baking paper.

Sift together the flours, bicarbonate of soda and salt into a large bowl and make a well in the centre. Add the buttermilk, treacle and honey and use a fork to start to bring everything together to form a wet dough.

Transfer the mixture from the bowl on to a lightly floured surface and knead it lightly before shaping it into a round.

Transfer the dough round to the lined baking tray. With a sharp knife, cut a deep cross in the top of the dough. This is so that when it bakes it will form naturally into quarters.

Bake the dough for 35 minutes, until it sounds hollow when tapped on the base. Remove the loaf from the oven and transfer it to a wire rack and leave it to cool.

Lockdown Sourdough

Everyone seemed to be making sourdough during the lockdown of 2020. This is Neil's lockdown sourdough recipe. The key to success was practice. It was a complete disaster the first time he made it but he's mastered it now.

   Luke Holder, my chef partner at our restaurant at Lime Wood, makes his bread in a Le Creuset, the heat acting like a clay oven. The bread that comes out is perfect. Now we make all our bread in a Le Creuset.

Males 2 x 1kg loaves

For the starter
500g strong white
   bread flour
20g runny honey

For the dough
400g active starter
   (see above)
900g strong white
   bread flour
100g wholemeal flour
20g salt

Stage 1: the starter
In a large bowl, mix 100g of the flour with 100ml of cold water and all the honey. Cover the bowl loosely with cling film and leave it in a draught-free, warm place for 24 hours.

After 24 hours, feed the starter by adding 200g more of the flour and 100ml of water and mixing well. Leave for 24–36 hours, after which you should see some movement – small bubbles of fermentation. At this point, feed the starter for a third and final time with the remaining 200g of flour and another 100ml of water. Mix well and leave the starter for a final 24 hours. After this, your starter should weigh about 800g and is ready to use.

Stage 2: the dough
Take half of your starter (400g) and refrigerate the other half for your next batch of sourdough. Put the starter you're using into a large mixing bowl. Add both flours to the bowl with the starter, along with the salt. Gradually incorporate everything together with 700ml of cold water until you form a dough. (You can do this by hand or in a stand mixer fitted with the dough hook, if you prefer.)

Tip the dough on to your work surface and knead it vigorously for 10–15 minutes, until the dough is smooth and elastic and comes away from the work surface. Shape the dough into a rough ball and place it back into a lightly floured bowl, cover with a cloth and allow it to rest for 45 minutes–1 hour.

In the meantime, prepare your baking baskets, making sure they are well floured. Gather a scalpel (or a very sharp knife) and two baking-paper cartouches – you can make these by cutting two sheets of baking paper into 25cm-diameter circles.

Tip the rested dough out on to your work surface and lift and stretch it 6 times to knead. Form it into a ball, transfer it back to the bowl and cover it with a damp cloth. Leave it to rest for a further 45 minutes.

Divide the dough into two 1kg balls and place them into your well-floured baskets, smooth side downwards. Cover and leave the dough to prove overnight in the fridge, or for 12 hours at room temperature.

Preheat the oven to 250°C/230°C fan/Gas 9–10 with two 25cm (9–10cm deep) heavy-based cast-iron pans, with lids, inside.

Tip each shaped loaf on to a cartouche and score a criss-cross into the top of the dough with a scalpel (or very sharp knife). Gently lift the loaves, on the baking paper, into the preheated pans and cover them with the lids. Bake for 20 minutes, until dark golden brown.

Tip the loaves gently on to a cooling rack and allow them to cool completely before slicing (if you can resist).

Conversion Charts

Weights

metric	imperial
15g	¹⁄₂oz
20g	³⁄₄oz
30g	1oz
55g	2oz
85g	3oz
110g	4oz / ¹⁄₄lb
140g	5oz
170g	6oz
200g	7oz
225g	8oz / ¹⁄₂lb
255g	9oz
285g	10oz
310g	11oz
340g	12oz / ³⁄₄ lb
370g	13oz
400g	14oz
425g	15oz
450g	16oz / 1lb
1kg	2lb 4oz
1.5kg	3lb 5oz

Liquids

metric	imperial
5ml	1 teaspoon
15ml	1 tablespoon or ¹⁄₂fl oz
30ml	2 tablespoons or 1fl oz
150ml	¹⁄₄ pint or 5fl oz
290ml	¹⁄₂ pint or 10fl oz
425ml	³⁄₄ pint or 16fl oz
570ml	1 pint or 20fl oz
1 litre	1³⁄₄ pints
1.2 litres	2 pints

Length

metric	imperial
5mm	¹⁄₄in
1cm	¹⁄₂in
2cm	³⁄₄ in
2.5cm	1in
5cm	2in
10cm	4in
15cm	6in
20cm	8in
30cm	12in

Useful conversions

1 tablespoon	= 3 teaspoons
1 level tablespoon	= approx. 15g or $\frac{1}{2}$oz
1 heaped tablespoon	= approx. 30g or 1oz

Oven temperatures

°C	°C Fan	Gas Mark	°F
110°C	90°C Fan	Gas Mark $\frac{1}{4}$	225°F
120°C	100°C Fan	Gas Mark $\frac{1}{2}$	250°F
140°C	120°C Fan	Gas Mark 1	275°F
150°C	130°C Fan	Gas Mark 2	300°F
160°C	140°C Fan	Gas Mark 3	325°F
180°C	160°C Fan	Gas Mark 4	350°F
190°C	170°C Fan	Gas Mark 5	375°F
200°C	180°C Fan	Gas Mark 6	400°F
220°C	200°C Fan	Gas Mark 7	425°F
230°C	210°C Fan	Gas Mark 8	450°F
240°C	220°C Fan	Gas Mark 9	475°F

Index

curried cauliflower, pine nuts and raisins 160
forgotten carrots 156
pea and sausage risotto 134
pumpkin, pear and walnut salad 42
puntarella with anchovy mayonnaise 48
radishes and anchovy mayonnaise 46
red cabbage with mackerel 110
roasted Italian peppers 142
summer vegetable soup 58
summer with poached chicken 74
turnip and celeriac gratin 162
see also artichokes; asparagus; aubergine;
   courgettes; fennel; mushrooms; onions;
   potatoes; radicchio
Victoria Sponge 224
vinaigrette mustard 36

W

walnuts pumpkin and pear salad 42
Whole Baked Turbot and Boiled Potatoes 116
Whole Trout with Almond and
   Herb Stuffing 114
wild garlic
   potato gnocchi and morels 128
   and potato soup 56

Thank You

My thanks to Jon at Absolute for his advice, patience and the long lunches, and to Emily – without her I would not be writing this.

Thank you to Tim, my agent, for making it happen in the first place, and to everyone who has worked on and contributed to the book: Meg Boas, Marie O'Shepherd, Peter Moffat, Anika Schulze, Judy Barratt, Elaine Byfield, Lisa Harrison, Rachel Malig, Zoe Ross, Maud Davies and Don Shanahan.

Of course huge love and thanks to Jonathan Lovekin, who just makes my food look so good. I love working with you.

Big thanks to all my neighbours who have entrusted me with their recipes, and to my friends Tony, Jane, Luca, George, Leone and Salvatore, as well as Welsh Jon, Henry, Denice and Annie, all of whom have been forced to eat and have their pictures taken in the process. Just one quick extra thanks to Randall; it was while working in New York in a chocolate shop and eating at the old school bakeries he came up with his incredible chocolate cake.

Thanks to Ben for your advice and corrections.

Thank you to Sandra for just being you, the pillar of our community.

Thanks to Jeremy for his photographs and his general enthusiasm for life.

And thank you to all the teams at the restaurants – Murano, Cafe Murano, Limewood and Portetta.

And last but by no means least, to Neil, my husband. Having worked for some incredible chefs, including Phil Howard, Michel Bras and Anne-Sophie Pic, he loves his Scottish roots and is still in touch with his first mentor and friend Chef Lyall. Many moons ago (about 20 years), Neil worked at the Connaught Hotel where we met. He made me laugh then and has never stopped… There's nothing better than sitting round a table with you, sharing food, wine and stories of life.

About the Author

Angela Hartnett, MBE, is one of the UK's most-loved chefs, known for her sophisticated yet simple Italian-inspired cooking. Born in Britain, her passion for food was instilled in her by her Italian grandmother and mother. Starting in the kitchens at Aubergine, Zafferano and L'Oranger, Angela became Head Chef at Petrus within seven months of starting there, helping the restaurant achieve a Michelin star. She went on to launch Verre in Dubai and Menu and The Grill Room at The Connaught with Gordon Ramsay.

In 2007 Angela was awarded an MBE for services to hospitality, and the following year she opened her own restaurant, Murano, where she is Chef Proprietor and holds a Michelin star. In 2012 Angela joined with Robin Hutson and chef Luke Holder to open Hartnett Holder & Co. Later that same year, Angela opened Cafe Murano, the little sister to Murano, which has been followed by two others, all based in London.

Angela is a regular face on British television, often appearing on *Saturday Kitchen* and as one of the judges on BBC's *Best Home Cook*. During the Covid pandemic, Angela was a key figurehead and spokesperson for the hospitality industry. This is her third book.

Publisher
Jon Croft

Commissioning Editor
Meg Boas

Senior Editor
Emily North

Art Direction
Marie O'Shepherd and Peter Moffat

Designer
Anika Schulze

Production Controller
Laura Brodie

Photographer
Jonathan Lovekin

Street party photographer
Jeremy Freedman and Angela Hartnett

Food Styling
Angela Hartnett and Neil Borthwick

Copyeditor
Judy Barratt

Home Economist
Elaine Byfield and Lisa Harrison

Proofreader
Rachel Malig

Indexer
Zoe Ross

BLOOMSBURY ABSOLUTE
Bloomsbury Publishing Plc
50 Bedford Square, London, WC1B 3DP, UK
29 Earlsfort Terrace, Dublin 2, Ireland

BLOOMSBURY, BLOOMSBURY ABSOLUTE, the Diana logo and the Absolute Press logo are trademarks of Bloomsbury Publishing Plc.

First published in Great Britain 2022

A catalogue record for this book is available from the British Library.
Library of Congress Cataloguing-in-Publication data has been applied for.

HB: 9781472975010
ePUB: 9781472975034
ePDF: 9781472975027

2 4 6 8 10 9 7 5 3 1

Printed in China by C&C Offset Printing Ltd.

To find out more about our authors and books visit
www.bloomsbury.com and sign up for our newsletters.